POTATO

Edible

Series Editor: Andrew F. Smith

EDIBLE is a revolutionary new series of books dedicated to food and drink that explores the rich history of cuisine. Each book reveals the global history and culture of one type of food or beverage.

Already published

Potato

A Global History

Andrew F. Smith

REAKTION BOOKS

Published by Reaktion Books Ltd
33 Great Sutton Street
London EC1V 0DX, UK
www.reaktionbooks.co.uk

First published 2011

Printed and bound in China by C&C Offset Printing Co. Ltd

British Library Cataloguing in Publication Data

Smith, Andrew F., 1946–
Potato: a global history. – (Edible)
1. Potatoes – History. 2. Potato products – History.
3. Cooking (Potatoes)
I. Title II. Series
641.3 521-DC22

ISBN: 978 1 86189 799 2

Contents

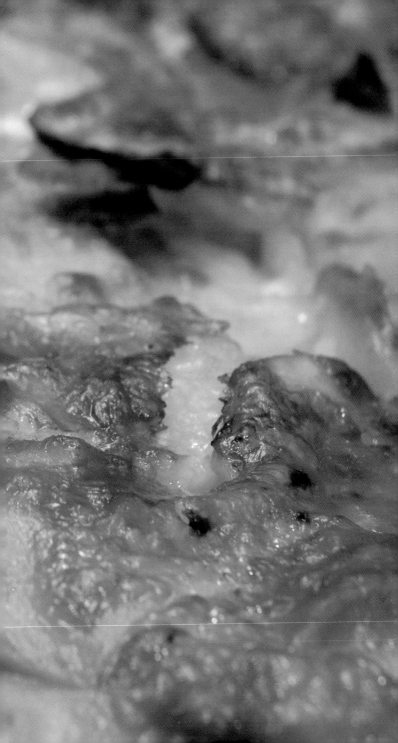

Introduction

The potato's history is a rags-to-riches story, from its obscure beginnings in the Andes mountains of South America in pre-Columbian times to its global stardom today. There are many reasons for the potato's success: it thrives at high altitudes and in arid climates where other staple crops, such as wheat, rice and corn (maize) can't grow; it has a fairly short growing season (75 days); and it requires relatively little effort to cultivate and harvest, for which the only tool needed is a spade – for planting, weeding and digging up the potatoes.

Potatoes are also prolific. A single plant produces an average of 4.4 pounds (2 kg) of potatoes, but productivity can be much greater. The *Guinness World Records* credits the Englishman Eric Jenkins with growing more than 370 lb (168 kg) of potatoes from a single tuber.

Then there's the potato's nutritional content. A medium-sized raw potato contains a mere one hundred calories and is a good source of vitamins C and B6, and of minerals including iron, potassium and zinc. If the skin is eaten, the potato is an excellent source of dietary fibre. Potatoes contain no fat or cholesterol, and are also low in sodium. They are a fine component of a healthful, balanced diet if they are prepared simply and sauced or flavoured with ingredients

Mashed potato soda.

that are low-fat or fat-free such as yoghurt, onions, herbs or salsa.

The potato is easily transported, and keeps well for months if stored properly. It is low-cost and adaptable to a tremendous variety of dishes featuring all sorts of tastes, textures and aromas. Potatoes can be boiled, baked, fried, roasted, steamed, sautéed, mashed, hashed, souffléed and scalloped. They are used in pancakes, dumplings, salads, soups, stews, chowders and savoury puddings. Due to this versatility, more potatoes are consumed than any other vegetable, and in terms of international production, potatoes rank behind only wheat and rice as the most important food in the world.

As important as the potato is today, hundreds of years were to pass after Europeans first ran into the spud in South America in the mid-sixteenth century before it was widely adopted in the mid-nineteenth century in Europe. It was not generally consumed in China, today the world's largest potato producer, until the mid-twentieth century. The potato's path to stardom began about 12,000 years ago.

I

The Wild and
Domesticated Potato

The traditional view of human settlement in the Americas is that indigenous peoples crossed the Bering Straits 16,000 years ago and moved rapidly down the west coast of the Americas, reaching Monte Verde in southern Chile about 14,000 years ago.[1] These early Americans were hunters and gatherers, and they were sustained by a vast variety of edible wild plants. Among these were 235 different species of potatoes, which inhabited a wide expanse of territory encompassing most of South America as well as Central America and the American Southwest. Of all the domesticated food plants in the world today, none boasts as large a group of wild ancestors as the potato.

The western coast of South America has a narrow desert intersected by valleys carved out by rivers originating a short distance away, in the Andes, one of the world's longest and highest mountain ranges. The eastern side of the Andes gradually slopes into dense tropical rainforests. Within this fragmented geography, numerous microclimates and a wide range of environments can be found, from deserts and fertile river valleys to jungles and glaciers.

The Andes have little flat land or fertile soil, but indigenous farmers terraced mountainsides, constructed irrigation ditches and domesticated an estimated seventy plants – almost as many plants as were domesticated in all of Europe or Asia. Twenty-five were tuber or root crops, such as the peppery-tasting *añu* or *mashua* (*Tropaeolum tuberosum*), the radish-like *maca* (*Lepidium meyenii*), the brightly coloured *oca* (*Oxalis tuberosa*) and the *ulluco* (*Ullucus tuberosus*), as well as seven potato species, the most important being *Solanum tuberosum*. Many root plants are still grown commercially in South America today, but only one, *S. tuberosum* – the common potato – was catapulted from obscurity to global importance.

Domestication of *S. tuberosum* was likely accomplished around 10,000 BCE by Andean farmers, probably in the Lake Titicaca basin. In one of the world's most inhospitable terrains for agriculture, the potato became the chief food of the people. The potato was well suited to the warm days of summer, which encouraged the growth of the above-ground plant, and the cold nights encouraged the growth of the tuber. Through trial and error, Andean farmers concluded that potatoes could be propagated by seed or by planting sprouts from its tubers. Not all potato plants produce seed balls, which are about the size of a cherry tomato. Growing plants from seeds produced a vast array of shapes, colours, sizes and tastes, but when a farmer found a type of potato he liked, he perpetuated the strain by planting the tubers, which are clones of the original plant. In this way, pre-Columbian peoples grew about 200 varieties of potatoes, and thousands more have been subsequently developed, making potatoes one of the world's most diverse domesticated crops.

The most important domesticated potato in the Andes was *S. t. andigena*. Daylight-sensitive, it could only be grown near the equator, where night and day were about equal in duration. Its tubers were large, and tended to be round and uniform, with deep 'eyes' and a high starch content. They

Chuño is a way of storing dried potatoes developed by prehistoric people in the Andes.

were grown on small communal fields in valleys and terraces on the mountainsides. Farmers fertilized the crop with manure provided by their beasts of burden, the llama and alpaca. Different varieties of potatoes were planted at different elevations, which made it possible for farmers to plant and harvest potatoes throughout the year. To plant potatoes in rocky soil, farmers used wooden spades and digging sticks, hardened by fire and sometimes tipped with copper. To harvest potatoes, farmers used hand axes.

Once harvested, potatoes, even under ideal conditions, keep for only a few months before they sprout, and they are vulnerable to mould and decay. Indigenous South Americans, however, developed a method of preserving them so that they could be stored for years to provide a safeguard against famine. The chill, arid climate of the *altiplano* (the high Andean plateau) made this possible. After harvest, the potatoes were covered to prevent dew from settling on them and left out overnight in freezing temperatures. The following day, the potatoes were exposed to the sun and farm families – men, women and children alike – trod on the frozen potatoes to express their liquid, a process repeated several times during the following days. The resulting freeze-dried potato, called *chuño*, was stored in sealed, permanently frozen underground warehouses where it would keep for years before deteriorating. *Chuño* was ground into flour and baked into bread, or rehydrated and used for thickening soups and stews, such as *chupe*, which was made with available meat and vegetables. Potatoes and *chuño* were carried down from the *altiplano* on the backs of llamas to lower elevations, where they were bartered in markets for maize, manioc, coca and other staples. *Chuño* was also placed in the graves of the pre-Columbian Chimú as a way of feeding the dead on their journey in the afterlife.

Andean civilizations emerged 4,500 years ago. Depictions of potatoes have been found on pottery of this period, including pieces from the Moche, Chimú, Nazca and other pre-Columbian civilizations that flourished and disappeared before the advent of the Inca, initially a small tribe living around Cuzco. In 1200 CE the Inca founded a small kingdom that gradually absorbed adjacent peoples in the Andes

Today, *chuño* is still made by the Quechua and Aymara communities of Peru and Bolivia.

mountains. Beginning in the mid-fifteenth century the Inca began a rapid expansion through a series of conquests. At its zenith, the Inca empire extended 2,000 miles, from what is today central Chile to southern Colombia, and had a population of nine to fifteen million diverse peoples. The Inca called their empire *Tahuantinsuyu*, the Kingdom of Four Corners – coast, plateau, mountain and jungle. Within the Inca empire land was cultivated in common. No taxes were paid, but men were required to work on civic projects, such as the construction of roads, fortresses, monuments, temples and a vast infrastructure of roads and footpaths that allowed for rapid communications and commercial activity within their empire. Workers also constructed and managed vast government storehouses that were stocked with enough *chuño* to prevent

Potatoes after freezing and drying, the common *chuño* of Peru and Bolivia.

Specimen of *chuño* of a better quality, known as a *tunta*.

famine for several years. The most important crop in the Inca Empire was potatoes, which in Quechua, the main language of the Inca, were called 'papas'.

The Spanish Encounter with the Potato

For all its size and grandeur, the Inca Empire lasted only a century before it was conquered by the Spanish, beginning in 1532. Even before the Spanish Conquistadores arrived in central South America, the Inca had begun to suffer from the European arrival in the New World, for the Europeans brought diseases with them that peoples in the Americas had no immunity to. Shortly after Europeans landed in South America, smallpox, measles, typhoid, influenza, malaria, whooping cough and other diseases decimated the indigenous peoples of the Americas. These Old World diseases spread to the Inca Empire by the 1520s. Just before the arrival of the Spanish in the Andes, epidemics killed many Inca leaders, including their Emperor and his successor. Eventually an estimated one-third to one-half of the total population of the Inca Empire died of these viral killers. Those who survived were demoralized, which contributed to the relatively easy Spanish conquest of the Inca.

Francisco Pizarro and his expedition were likely the first Europeans to encounter the potato. Pizarro had come to the New World around 1502. He sailed with Vasco Núñez de Balboa, whose expedition crossed the Isthmus of Panama and sighted the Pacific Ocean. Pizarro subsequently became *alcalde* (mayor) of the newly established Spanish colony of Panama City. In 1522 a Spanish explorer returned from exploring central Colombia with reports of a gold-rich empire on a river called Pirú (later corrupted to Perú). This story greatly interested Pizarro. Two years later he launched the first of two unsuccessful expeditions along the western coast of South America in search of this supposedly rich empire. In 1532 Pizarro made a third attempt by landing two hundred Conquistadores in Peru. This time he was successful in conquering the Inca Empire with its 80,000 armed and disciplined troops.

Despite Pizarro's inevitable contact with potatoes, neither he nor his men wrote about them. The first Spanish record of the potato appears a few years later, when Jiménez de Quesada led an expedition from Santa Marta, on the Caribbean coast, into the interior of New Granada (today Colombia). In 1537 his forces captured Bogotá, then the capital of the Chibcha kingdom. According to Juan de Castellanos, who wrote *Historia del Nuevo Reino de Granada*, in the Valle de la Grita near the modern border with Ecuador, the expedition found 'truffles' with little round roots 'the size of an egg, more or less, some round and others oblong; they are white and purple and yellow, floury roots with a good taste, a very acceptable gift for the Indians and even a treat for the Spanish'. Although written after 1601, this description was likely based on an actual account of the expedition, and it is considered the first located reference to the potato.

Two published accounts of potatoes appeared in the early 1550s. Pedro Cieza de León, who went to Peru in 1532 (but didn't write down an account of his adventures until 1550), mentions *papas* as a staple food of the Inca in his *Parte primera de la crónica del Peru* (1553). Francisco López de Gómara in his *Historia General de las Indias* (1553), wrote that in Bolivia the men ate roots similar to truffles, 'which they call papas'.

Garcilaso de la Vega, the son of an Inca princess and a Spanish father, born in Cuzco in 1539, disclosed in his *Royal Commentaries of the Incas* that potatoes ('*pappas*') were the principal food – they served as the Incan bread. They could also

Poma de Ayala's illustrations of Incas harvesting potatoes from his early 17th-century manuscript. A man is raising the crop with a *tacalla*, and women are breaking the clods with a hook and carrying the crop to store.

be boiled or roasted and put into stews. Another rare example of such an account was written by Poma de Ayala, the son of a noble Inca family. In the late sixteenth century he began compiling a manuscript about life in Peru under Spanish rule. Around 1615, he sent it to the Spanish royal court, where it was lost for three centuries. Poma de Ayala makes numerous references to potatoes, and reports that there were many varieties: 'Potatoes can be large or small, new or early-maturing, flat in shape, white and delicate, frozen or preserved.' He included illustrations of Inca planting, ploughing, cultivating and harvesting potatoes.

When José de Acosta, a Jesuit priest, was sent to Peru from Spain in 1571, he read all the material then available on the Americas. Once in the New World he began recording extensive notes based on his own observations, eventually compiling his *Historia natural y moral de las Indias*, first published in 1590. In this work Acosta reports that potatoes were the Indians' main food. A fuller account was recorded by Bernabé Cobo, a Jesuit missionary in Peru during the early seventeenth century, who also compiled a natural history. In 1653 Cobo wrote that potatoes could be eaten raw when freshly dug, or, after storage, roasted or used in stews. If not eaten soon after they were harvested, Cobo observed, potatoes were preserved through a process of dehydration accomplished by freezing and exposure to the sun. Cobo noted that *chuño* was toasted and then ground into flour.

Chilean Potatoes

The potato was also domesticated in central Chile. This variety, today called *Solanum tuberosum tuberosum*, was not daylight-sensitive and it grew in coastal areas of southern South

America, as well as on the Chiloé Archipelago, off the coast of Chile. When the British privateer Sir Francis Drake visited Chiloé in 1577, on his two-year circumnavigation of the world, he bartered potatoes from the natives. According to a wide variety of sources, Drake brought the potatoes on board his ship, carried them across the Pacific and around the Horn of Africa, and was the first person to introduce them into Northern Europe. Redcliffe Salaman, in his *History and Social Influence of the Potato*, debunked this myth by noting that the potatoes would have rotted long before the voyage was over. Of course, it is entirely possible that European travellers brought potato seeds on board, but Salaman pointed out that in all early accounts of potato propagation the plants were grown from tubers.

Salaman concluded that *S. t. tuberosum* didn't arrive in Europe much before the mid-seventeenth century, and that it wasn't commonly grown until the early nineteenth century. Despite this late start, virtually all potatoes grown outside the Americas today are of this variety. *S. t. andigena* is grown commercially only on mountaintops from Argentina to Venezuela and in Central America and Mexico.

The Potato Changes World History

After the Conquest, the Spanish continued to encourage the potato's cultivation, and to collect taxes in the form of *chuño*, which the Spanish used to feed workers who built roads, churches and cities. Workers in silver mines were fed almost exclusively on *chuño*. In 1546 the Spanish discovered a rich deposit of silver ore in a mountain in Potosí, Bolivia, and they impressed tens of thousands of indigenous peoples to mine the ore. Many of these workers died of ill-treatment and from mercury poisoning. With indigenous labour becoming scarce, the Spanish imported 30,000 African slaves to work the mines. About eight million natives and slaves are estimated to have died as a result of their work in the Potosí mines. Between 1556 and 1783, more than 45,000 US tons (40,800 metric tons) of silver were mined, and much of it was shipped to the Spanish monarchy.

This tragic story led historian William McNeill to observe that potatoes paid for Spain's military conquests and political power in the sixteenth and seventeenth centuries, and thus the potato, which fed the workers, had radically changed world history. Potatoes would change history again, proclaimed McNeill, in the mid-eighteenth century, when they provided the fuel for the rapid population growth of Northern Europe – and it was this massive rise in population that permitted Western European nations to colonize the world.

2

The Potato Diaspora

Spanish explorers encountered many new plants in the Caribbean, among them one with a tuberous root, called by the Taino Indians *batatas*. The Indians roasted these roots and also made bread from them, and once the Spaniards tasted these starchy staples they sent home enthusiastic reports of their discovery. No less an explorer than Christopher Columbus himself described the root as resembling a yam (*Dioscorea*) and tasting like a chestnut. An early sixteenth-century account proclaimed that they 'haue the taste of rawe chestnuttes, but are sumwhat sweeter'. Another visitor to the Caribbean reported that when *batatas* were well cured they tasted just like marzipan. Yet another Spanish writer claimed that when roasted, they tasted honey-sweet. The plant was fast growing and the roots could be stored for a few months, which made them ideal for ships' stores. Moreover, the Spanish fancied *batatas* an aphrodisiac, and so the tubers were among the first New World foods adopted in Europe.

The first Englishman to write about the newly discovered plant was the slaver and adventurer John Hawkins, who encountered *patatas* in the Caribbean in 1565. Hawkins changed the spelling to *potatoes* and called them 'the most delicate rootes that may be eaten'. Comparing them to familiar

European vegetables, he opined that they 'doe far exceede our passeneps or carets'. Potatoes could not easily be grown in the British Isles at the time, but by 1576 a regular trade in them flourished between England and the Iberian peninsula. William Harrison, in his *Description of England* (1577), claimed that potatoes were 'venerous roots' – that is, an aphrodisiac. Thomas Dawson's *The Good Huswives Iewell* (1587) includes a recipe for 'Potatum', which, he assures the reader, will 'give courage to a man or woman'. In Shakespeare's play *The Merry Wives of Windsor* (1598), the Bard writes, 'Let the sky rain potatoes' – yet another reference to their aphrodisiac qualities. These coveted tubers were, in fact, sweet potatoes

The sweet potato plant and tuber, print, 1800–1860.

(*Ipomoea batatas*), which are not botanically related to the common potato. When Europeans came into contact with *Solanum tuberosum*, however, they gave it the same name and credited it with the same aphrodisiac qualities, and this contributed to the white potato's relatively rapid dissemination throughout the late sixteenth and seventeenth centuries.

The common potato arrived in Europe some time before 1573, when the first reference to it appeared in a hospital account book in Seville, Spain. What is unclear is precisely where these potatoes came from. Potatoes stored in ships sailing from the west coast of South America would have rotted well before they arrived in Europe. Historian Redcliffe Salaman provided a solution to this riddle. Salaman pointed out in *The History and Social Influence of the Potato* that although they were not grown in the Caribbean, by 1549 potatoes grown in the Andes of Colombia were traded at markets in Cartagena, on the Caribbean coast. Potatoes were ideal for feeding sailors on long voyages, but when the ships arrived in Spain, excess provisions would have been jettisoned. So it's not surprising that the first record of *S. tuberosum* outside of South America appears in the Canary Islands, a stopping point for ships sailing to and from the Americas. Potatoes were exported from the Canary Islands to Europe by the 1560s.

Andigena potatoes – those domesticated in Peru – grew best in cool and moist climates and thus would not have thrived in hot, dry areas of southern Spain, yet this is where the first known reference to the potato in Europe appears. Shortly after their arrival in Spain, potatoes were sent to Italy, where they were at first called *taratouffli* (truffles) for their superficial resemblance to that precious commodity. As the potato became more common in countries to the north and east, variations on the original Italian name came into use. It was called *tarteuffel* in Swiss, *cartoufle* in old French, *Taratouphli* (later *Kartoffel*) in German and *Картошка* in Russian.

Thanks to the riches of the Americas, especially silver from Peru's Potosí mines, the Spanish were able to equip armies mighty enough to dominate much of Europe for almost a century. When the Spanish engaged in war in the Low Countries, they developed a supply line that ran from Spain through northern Italy, south-western Germany and south-eastern France to what is today Belgium. The Spanish armies brought potatoes with them, and farmers along the supply line grew potatoes to sell to the military formations and supply trains as they passed by. Potatoes were grown in Italy by the 1570s, in Germany by 1581 and in Switzerland, France and the Low Countries shortly thereafter.

By the seventeenth century the potato was cultivated as an agricultural crop, especially as a substitute for rye. It made an excellent rotation crop: rather than letting land lie fallow for a year, farmers planted potatoes, which took different nutrients from the soil, attracted different insects and controlled weeds. Although they did not know it at the time, potatoes also had superior food value, supplying about four times the calories of rye by weight. The potato plant was well adapted to northern European conditions: it could be grown in differing soil conditions; was easy to cultivate with hand tools; took only three to four months to mature; and supplied a bountiful crop of highly nutritious food.

How and when potatoes reached England has been a matter of conjecture. Francis Drake is reported to have introduced potatoes from Chile into England in 1578. He did acquire potatoes from natives off the coast of Chile, but these would not have survived his return trip home as he circumnavigated the globe. That said, Drake did sack Cartagena (today in Colombia) in 1586. Potatoes were clearly available in the city, but no record has been located that indicates that he stocked up on them as a provision for his fleet or brought them back to England when he returned a few months later. A second myth was that Walter Raleigh brought potatoes back to England from the Caribbean in 1588, and then cultivated them on his estate in Ireland. Raleigh did not visit the Caribbean in the sixteenth century, although he did fund expeditions to Roanoke Island, which established the first English settlement in North America. But potatoes were not grown in North America at the time.

The first published work unmistakably to mention the common potato was John Gerard's *Catalogus Arborum* in 1596. Gerard offered two Latin names for potatoes: *Papus orbiculatus* ('disk-shaped' or 'rounded') and *Papus Hyspanorum* ('Spanish'). When he revised the *Catalogus* in 1599, he also supplied English names: 'Bastard Potatoes' and 'Spanish Potatoes'. In Gerard's *Great Herball, or Generall Historie of Plantes*, published in 1597, he wrote that he had grown potatoes in his garden and that they grew

> as in their owne natiue countrie. The Indians do call this plant Papus (meaning the rootes), by which name also the common potatoes are called in those Indian countries. We haue the name proper vnto it mentioned in the title, bicause it hath not only the shape and proportion of potatoes, but also the pleasant taste and virtues of the same. We may call it in English, Potatoes of America or Virginia.

In fact, no potatoes were being grown in Virginia at the time, so either Gerard got the location wrong or he misidentified the plant. The Jerusalem artichoke (*Helianthus tuberosus*), then very popular in Europe, and many other plants with tubers did grow in eastern North America, and perhaps he just confused them.

John Gerard (1545–1607), frontispiece to the first edition of the *Great Herball*, 1597.

Gerard received some of his information about the potato – and perhaps his potatoes themselves – from the Flemish botanist and herbalist Charles de l'Escluse (Carolus Clusius). According to Clusius, in 1587 Philippe de Sivry, Lord of Walhain and Governor of the town of Mons in Belgium, received some common potatoes from the Papal Legate in that country. De Sivry sent two tubers to Clusius, who at the

John Gerard, 'Virginian Potato', from the *Herball* of 1597 – the first known illustration of the potato.

time was studying plants in Vienna; Clusius identified them as *Papas peruanum*. By 1590 potatoes were growing in Breslau (today Wrocław, Poland) and the first illustration of the potato derives from here.

It was the Swiss botanist Caspar Bauhin who gave the potato its 'correct' scientific name, *Solanum tuberosum*, in his *Phytopinax*, published in 1597. Bauhin later expanded this to a trinomial: *S. t. tuberosum*. Bauhin's term was used by Carl Linnaeus as the potato's official name in 1753. The '*Solanum tuberosum* Group Tuberosum' refers to the potato variety that originated in coastal Chile. These are smooth-skinned and watery. The Spanish did not complete their conquest of Chile until 1565, and regular shipping through the Straits of Magellan did not begin until almost a century later, so it is unlikely that *S. t. tuberosum* was shipped back to Europe until the eighteenth century. As it was grown far south of the equator, it could also be grown in northern Europe during the summer, but this variety did not become an important commercial variety until the early nineteenth century.

Not all herbalists saw the potato as an important addition to the European food supply. In fact, several were convinced that potatoes were poisonous and caused leprosy, dysentery and other diseases. Some French provincial governments, such as those in Franche-Comté and Burgundy, forbade their

Solanum tuberosum esculentum – potato from Bauhin, *Prodromos*, 1620.

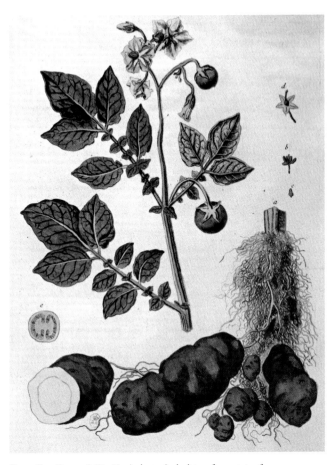

Geneviève Regnault De Nagis, botanical plate of a potato, from
'La Botanique Mise à la portée de tout le Monde', c. 1774.

cultivation. The French agricultural expert Olivier de Serres
noted in his *Le théâtre d'agriculture et mésnage* of 1600 that *Cartoufle*, with fruit similar to truffles, had recently arrived from
Switzerland, but that the taste was little different than other
root crops. Elsewhere in Europe it was suggested that the

potato would have been mentioned in the Bible had it been intended to be eaten. These negative views survived in some parts of Europe almost until the end of the eighteenth century.

Potatoes were grown in parts of Germany by the early seventeenth century, and they were field crops in the Palatinate and in Alsace by 1660. In the latter part of the century French armies marching into the Rhineland encountered the potato, but it wasn't until the War of the Spanish Succession (1701–14) that the potato became an essential commissary item. This war produced one of the worst famines in European history, and by 1709 peasants and soldiers alike adopted the potato without hesitation. By 1715 potatoes were grown as field crops throughout the Low Countries, the Rhine Valley, south-west Germany and eastern France. Potatoes were cultivated in the gardens of Danish and Swedish aristocrats by the 1730s, and in lower-class gardens by the 1770s. By 1800 potatoes had become a field crop in Denmark and Sweden.

A subsequent famine in 1740 moved Prussia's Frederick the Great to encourage potato cultivation by publicizing the tubers and giving away potato seeds to farmers. After the famine of 1770–72, Prussia, Silesia, Poland and other countries became major potato producers.

Catherine the Great, Empress of Russia, observed this success and embarked on a systematic promotional campaign to encourage peasants to grow the crop. Although this was initially of limited success, the potato grew easily in Russia and it could be used as a great substitute for making bread if the wheat crop failed. By 1800 potatoes were cultivated in the western parts of Russia and the Ukraine. Russia expanded its production of potatoes throughout the nineteenth century, and the crop became central to Russian cuisine. Russians used potatoes for a variety of culinary purposes, and they quickly became Russia's most popular vegetable.

In England, Scotland and Ireland, potatoes were mainly grown in gardens until the late seventeenth century. In England potatoes, especially the Lumper variety, produced large crops but didn't taste great. They were used as horse fodder in England, but in Scotland and Ireland they were grown for human consumption. By 1664 potatoes had become so important that John Forester concluded in his book, *Englands Happiness Increased*, that planting potatoes was a sure preventive of future famine; for thirty pounds of potatoes could be produced on one acre of land.

By 1699 potato cultivation had spread all over Britain and Ireland and one observer called the 'wholesome and nourishing roots' a great 'resource for the people of England'. During the following century potatoes increasingly found favour throughout England as a commercial field crop. Adam Smith, in his *Wealth of Nations*, published in 1776, nominated maize and potatoes as 'the two most important improvements which the agriculture of Europe . . . has received from the great extension of its commerce and navigation'.

Although potatoes had arrived in the south-eastern part of France by the late sixteenth century, they were grown mainly as a garden vegetable until the mid-eighteenth century, when they became a fairly common comestible. Even then, potatoes were not much appreciated by the ruling classes, and most potatoes were fed to farm animals. Denis Diderot's respected *Encyclopédie* (1765–76) proclaimed that the potato, 'no matter how one cooks it is insipid and starchy . . . one blames and with reason, for its windiness, but what is a question of wind to the virile organs of the peasant and the worker?'

The potato's eventual rise to prominence in France can be credited in part to Antoine-Augustin Parmentier, a pharmacist who fought in the French army during the Seven Years

War (1756–63). He was captured and spent five years as a prisoner of war in Germany, where he and his fellow prisoners subsisted mainly on potatoes. Like many other Frenchmen, he had never eaten them before. Parmentier survived his imprisonment and became a great believer in the nutritional properties of the potato; back home in France, he championed potatoes as food for humans. After the French grain harvest failed in 1769, the Academy at Besançon launched a competition to identify alternatives to grains. Parmentier wrote a treatise on potatoes that won the contest. In 1773 Parmentier published *Examen chymique des pommes de terre*, which convincingly promoted the nutritional value of potatoes. That same year he was appointed pharmacist at the Hôtel-des-Invalides and moved to Paris, where he continued his potato campaign. In Paris Parmentier met Benjamin Franklin, who was trying to drum up French support for the American War for Independence. Parmentier told Franklin about his campaign to promote the potato, and Franklin suggested tendering a dinner for prominent Frenchmen with all the courses, from soup to dessert, made from potatoes. The dinner, which was attended by Franklin and Antoine Lavoisier, another prominent scientist, was held on 29 October 1778; the menu included a 'fish' dish made from potatoes and toasts with potato vodka. Franklin made a point of praising the meal in his letters and public pronouncements.

During this period, grain harvests were low and bread prices were high. This particularly affected the poor. Parmentier spent considerable effort trying to encourage bakers to substitute the inexpensive potato starch for flour. Potatoes and potato starch can be a good addition to bread-making, but the amounts that Parmentier advocated produced bread that was distasteful. As Barbara K. Wheaton, author of *Savoring the Past: The French Kitchen and Table from 1300 to 1789* (1996),

A 1913 commemorative edition of *Le Petit Journal* celebrating 'The centenary of a benefactor of humanity', Antoine-Augustin Parmentier.

Le centenaire d'un bienfaiteur de l'humanité
PARMENTIER PROPAGATEUR DE LA POMME DE TERRE EN FRANCE

concluded, he may well have delayed the acceptance of the potato in France, where it was relegated mainly to being a source of starch, fodder for animals and a food for the poor.

Despite Parmentier's efforts, it took some time before the general public began to accept the new food crop, which occurred as the nineteenth century progressed. By 1815 the nation produced 21 million hectolitres of potatoes; by 1840 it had risen to 117.

Potatoes required little effort to grow, harvest and consume, and were mainly grown by lower classes. Aristocrats considered potato-eaters lazy and irresponsible. As potatoes were abundant and relatively nutritious, potato-growing

Potato organizations developed postcards, such as this one from Canada, 'Potatoes grow big here', to gain visibility and promote sales.

supported large families, and population explosions occurred wherever potatoes became a major crop. Between 1750 and 1850 Europe's population grew from about 140 million to 266 million, and several historians attribute this growth in part to the vast increase in potato-growing during this time.

As the potato can be stored for a few months before it dries out or rots, it was perfect for ships' stores. The potato had another advantage: although the sailors did not know it, potatoes contain a considerable amount of vitamin C, and when eaten raw are a deterrent to scurvy. Hence crews in ships with potatoes had a better chance of survival on long voyages. If the potatoes were not all consumed on their voyage, they would have been dumped out when they reached their destination. In this way the potato was introduced many times to different places in the Americas, the Pacific islands and Asia.

Although potatoes arrived in North America in the late 1600s, they did not become a field crop until the middle of the following century, when Scotch-Irish immigrants brought potatoes to New England from Ireland. Potatoes spread from there to the other regions. Subsequent immigrants from Germany, Scandinavia and Eastern Europe also grew and consumed potatoes. By the mid-nineteenth century, potatoes were an important field crop in Canada and the United States.

From Europe, potato culture spread south and east. Potatoes were introduced into Africa, where they became staples in the Atlas Mountains of North Africa, the Jos Plateau of Nigeria and the mountainous areas of east Africa. From Russia potatoes were disseminated to Turkey's Anatolian plateau and to western China. Simultaneously, European explorers took potatoes across the Pacific. The potato was brought to Japan, Korea and eastern China in the seventeenth century, but did not attract much interest: of the New World foods that arrived in China, potatoes were initially one of the least successful. Eventually they were grown in mountainous areas, particularly in the western part of the country. The British introduced potatoes into the South Pacific, and the plants grew well in Australia and New Zealand, where by 1805 potatoes were being grown as a field crop by Maoris. The British also introduced potatoes into India, where they were cultivated in mountainous areas, especially the Punjab.

In the late twentieth century production of potatoes in India and China increased to the point that China reigned as the largest producer and India was the third largest in the world, a position both countries have held ever since. By the twentieth century, the potato was the single most cultivated and consumed vegetable in the world.

3
The European Potato Famine

In the late summer of 1842 farmers around Philadelphia noticed something amiss with their potato plants: first, the leaves curled, then the body of the plant wilted. When dug up, the tubers were found to be penetrated by brown streaks; later, the potatoes turned into a slimy, blackened mass. What caused the disease was unknown, but it could wipe out a farmer's potato crop in a matter of days and the blight rapidly spread west throughout Pennsylvania and north to New York and Massachusetts. The 'potato rot', as it was called, received extensive coverage in the gardening and agricultural press. For most Americans in the 1840s, potatoes were a common food, but few depended on them as their sole sustenance. Most farmers who grew potatoes simply shifted to other crops, so the rot had little effect on most Americans.

In June 1844 the late potato blight appeared in Belgium. The following month, it was discovered in the Netherlands, and then it quickly spread to Scandinavian countries, France, western and southern Germany, Prussia and Russia. The blight devastated Dutch and Belgian potato farmers: an estimated 71 per cent of the Dutch potato crop and 88 per cent of the Belgian crop was destroyed. In France the blight was localized, and it affected fewer farmers. The French response was to send food from unaffected parts of their nation, and this response was well organized and effective. In some places, such as in southern Germany and Russia, farmers had grain crops to fall back on. In addition, European governments temporarily suspended their protectionist policies, making it possible to import cheap grain from other countries. But the results were particularly severe for those who relied solely on the potato harvest for their livelihood and sustenance. An estimated 300,000 Dutch, Belgian, Prussian and other rural farmers and their families died as result of the potato blight in continental Europe. Broader famine was forestalled in part due to European grain harvests, and the purchases of food from unaffected countries. Ireland, for instance, exported thousands of tons of potatoes during the summer of 1845 to help avert famine in continental Europe.

On 1 August 1845 the potato blight was recorded in the Channel Islands. Ten days later it was discovered in England, then Scotland and finally Ireland. Cognizant of its disastrous consequences in Belgium and Holland in 1844–5, political leaders in the United Kingdom took note and began to prepare for the worst. Sir Robert Peel, the British Prime Minister, appointed a Scientific Commission to study the blight and make recommendations; when they reported that there was no known way to prevent or cure the blight, and that the resulting loss would cause a major famine, Peel made preparations for defusing potential problems before they became crises. He introduced laws instituting public works projects which would give workers money to buy food. Half would be paid for by the British government and the rest supported by local funds; charity operations were set up in affected areas; local landlords were required to give relief to their tenants; and emergency hospitals were established.

The loss of the potato crop tended to be localized and limited in England, but the loss of the potato crop in the Highlands of Scotland was a serious problem. Landlords developed construction projects and set up relief efforts. Tenant farmers worked on public works projects and were able to buy food, which was available for those with money.

During the next few years, the effects of the potato blight on Europe and England were minor. Scotland's worst year, however, was 1849. While major famine was averted, an estimated one million Highlanders emigrated to England or North America. In Ireland, however, the blight caused a massive human tragedy.

The Irish Potato

Sir Walter Raleigh, an Englishman, has often been credited with introducing the potato into Ireland. Raleigh fought against a rebellion in Ireland from 1579 to 1581 and was rewarded with an estate in County Cork that had been confiscated from the Irish. There is no primary source evidence connecting Raleigh with potatoes, but a venerable chain of folklore links the two. The first version of the story appeared in 1693, when Sir Robert Southwell, president of the Royal Society, claimed that his grandfather, one Anthony Southwell, born in 1567, had acquired potatoes from Raleigh and planted them on his own estate, which was 25 miles from Raleigh's. In 1699 another member of the royal Society, John Houghton, claimed that Raleigh acquired the potatoes in Virginia and brought them to Ireland. Raleigh did fund four expeditions to America and did establish the earliest English settlement in America on Roanoke Island, but he never went to Virginia himself – and anyway, there were no potatoes in Virginia at the time.

But if Raleigh wasn't responsible, who was? Historian William McNeill speculated that it was more likely that a Spanish sailor brought potatoes from Spain – or perhaps a Basque fisherman brought them ashore to eat when he dried his catch in western Ireland. Whoever did the deed, potatoes were growing in Ireland by about 1600, although they were not common there for another fifty years.

Initially, potatoes were grown in gardens or on small plots. When the English conquered Ireland during the Cromwellian wars in the mid-seventeenth century, the Irish were pushed into the western part of the island, which was hilly with poor soil. This made most crop farming difficult, but the land was well suited for potatoes. Each plant yielded a great many tubers – an estimated six tons per acre – and, unlike grains, could be grown with little expense or effort. Growing potatoes did not require horses, oxen, ploughs or mills, just a spade and plenty of manual labour. In addition to providing food for the grower's family, the tuber could be fed to livestock – pigs, cows and poultry – and used to make starch and gin. Unlike many other vegetables, potatoes could be stored for several months if kept under the proper conditions. Then again, if a farmer produced more potatoes than his family could eat, the market for potatoes was stable. Finally, potatoes provided more well-rounded nourishment than the grain-based diets of the poor in England. When potatoes were eaten with milk or cheese, the combination supplied a good amount of protein as well as vitamins and minerals. During the eighteenth century, the potato became one of Ireland's foremost crops.

After Ireland's conquest, the English Protestants passed Penal Laws that prevented Catholics from voting, joining most professions or teaching. Education was controlled by the Church of England, and it excluded Catholics. More important still, the Penal Codes prevented Catholics from owning land, which had been divided up into large estates and given to English Protestant settlers. Under English control, Presbyterians from Scotland moved into Northern Ireland, which resembled the geography and climate of their home land. They grew potatoes, but they also grew oats, as they had done in Scotland. English army veterans and others settled in southern Ireland. The Catholic Relief Act of 1829 repealed many of the harsh Penal laws, but despite its passage, very little changed in Ireland during the next fifteen years.

At the highest level of Irish Catholic society were tenant farmers who rented parts of large estates owned by English Protestants. As the estate owners spent much of their time in England, tenant farmers often tended the owner's crops, especially grains, or herded the owner's cattle, which were raised extensively in southern Ireland. Tenant farmers grew potatoes for their own tables. At the middle level of Irish Catholic society were the cottagers, rural labourers who rented small parcels of land, which they usually planted with potatoes. At the bottom rung of society were the city day workers who bought their food with the money they earned from their work.

Unlike grains, potatoes could not be stored from year to year, so they had to be either eaten up or planted each season. The potato was also susceptible to many diseases, and dozens of crop failures caused by disease or weather conditions hit Ireland between 1700 and 1844. These failures often brought famine and death, but they were mainly localized or confined to a single year of shortages, and alternative crops provided sustenance for the fast-growing Irish population. During the years 1727–9 a serious potato crop failure hit rural areas of western Ireland. What to do about this Irish famine and the rapidly increasing Irish population was a problem frequently discussed in the English press. A Protestant clergyman named Jonathan Swift offered a solution in his satirical essay, 'A Modest Proposal for Preventing the Children of Poor People in Ireland from Being a Burden to their Parents or Country, and for Making Them Beneficial to the Public' (1729), suggesting that the Irish children be stewed, baked, roasted and boiled, and consumed as sustenance. Thankfully, the famine abated.

Despite other major crop failures and famines, the Irish population effectively tripled during the century before 1841. One-third of the population, especially in the western rural areas, became increasingly dependent on their potato patches for their subsistence.

During the summers, when the previous year's potatoes had been used up and the current crop had not yet matured, the Irish were forced to buy food on credit. As the population of the island tripled, so did the number of poor people. In addition, rents for farms, cottages and houses increased, while the amount of land cultivated by families declined. If their potato crops did not materialize, cottagers and labourers had no other crop to fall back on. Many families descended into poverty well before 1845. This large-scale dependence on a single food crop that was subject to periodic failure alarmed many observers. Neither the government, whose options were many, nor the rural Irish, whose options were few, paid any attention to the warnings.

The Irish Potato Famine

While continental European farmers were suffering from the potato blight, Ireland remained largely untouched. Tons of Irish potatoes and grains were exported during the summer of 1845 to help avert famine in continental Europe. Not until

41

Irish Pig Fair illustration, 1870. Pigs were fattened on potatoes and sold at fairs such as these; pig-raising fell sharply and pig fairs went into a decline when food became scarce.

the end of August 1845 was the blight discovered in Ireland, and it wasn't reported in newspapers until 9 September. It spread quickly throughout much of the country. By the end of October urgent warnings of potential famine in Ireland began to surface, and plans were in place to manage the crisis. In early November Prime Minister Peel ordered the secret purchase of £100,000 worth of Indian corn (maize) from the United States; the corn was expected to feed an estimated million people in Ireland for a few months.

The blight reduced the Irish potato harvest by about 30 per cent in 1845, causing localized problems, particularly in the west of Ireland, where the roads were often impassable. Still, there were few, if any, cases of death from starvation. The immediate consequence of the blight was that potatoes were consumed in greater quantities – those with potatoes chose to harvest and eat them rather than have them destroyed by the blight, and starving farmers were forced to eat the seed potatoes they had set aside to plant the following spring. Pigs and cows, which were usually fed potatoes, were slaughtered in greater than usual numbers that autumn, as there was nothing to feed them over the winter.

As past potato failures had a predictable pattern, those planning to avert catastrophe concluded that the famine would emerge in the spring and summer of 1846. Plans were undertaken to help famine victims. Local relief committees were organized, which were expected to raise money to buy relief supplies. A new plan to build roads and other public works was instituted in hopes that labourers could generate income to buy grain and other food. Hospitals were established to avoid the overcrowding problems that had been present in previous famines. As the price of staples started to rise, the government sold corn to keep the cost of all food down, so that labourers could afford to feed their families.

Unfortunately, the corn sold by the government had little nutritional value, especially when compared with potatoes. It was flint corn, which was very hard and had to be ground before it could be cooked or baked. There were not enough commercial mills in Ireland to grind the corn into meal, and the Irish poor didn't have the equipment to grind it themselves. The Irish, desperate for food, ate it in any way they could, and often suffered from dysentery as a result.

In general, though, the relief efforts were successful. The relief committees depended upon the largesse of the 80,000 landlords, many of whom were absentee Protestants who lived in England and had little interest in contributing funds to Irish Catholic charities. In addition, many landowners were hopelessly in debt and were unable to contribute funds for relief of their own tenants. But public works projects generated wages for labourers, relief agencies collected funds for local efforts, the sale of corn kept the price of food down and the hospitals handled those who were suffering from fever and other diseases. Few people died during winter of 1845–6, and it appeared that there was enough food to hold off mass starvation in the spring; the potato crop would be ready for harvesting during the summer and the crises would be soon over.

It soon became clear that the famine warnings had been overstated and there would be no famine in Ireland. Peel, a confirmed supporter of free trade, used the possibility of a famine to serve as a pretext to repeal the Corn Laws, which prevented the importation of cheap grain and thus buttressed the price of English grain. In theory, the repeal would permit the importation of low-cost foreign grain, but as the repeal took three years to go into effect, this had little influence on the crisis in Ireland. Repeal did have an effect in England: it was very unpopular, and Peel lost considerable political support trying to get it passed in Parliament.

In London, Peel's Tory government fell in June of 1846 and the new Whig government reversed its course in Ireland: the public works projects that Peel's government had paid half the costs of were to be continued, but only with local funds. The government also decided not to import or supply food. Their view was that the free market should determine the price and supply of food, and that the corn provided by the Tories had interfered with this process. The government did establish food depots, to be opened only as a last resort, and these distributed all the remaining maize from America.

A number of underlying problems went unnoticed. Only about 80 per cent of the former potato crop was planted in the spring of 1846 as many farmers did not have seed potatoes to plant. Some had lost their entire crop to the blight, while others had eaten their seed potatoes in order to survive during the winter. For those who had seed potatoes and planted

Daniel McDonald, *The Discovery of the Potato Blight in Ireland*, *c.* 1847.

them, the situation appeared hopeful. Early signs indicated that the potato crop was not infected by the blight, but the growers had planted their potatoes in infected ground. Climatic conditions, such as the mild winter of 1845–6, fostered the survival and spread of the potato blight; then extended rains and cold weather during the summer further increased the devastation of the blight, which spread at an estimated speed of 50 miles (80 km) per week. By July of 1846 the blight was virtually everywhere, and its destruction was comprehensive: 88 per cent of the Irish potato crop failed.

By this time the Whig government concluded that food needed to be purchased for Ireland, but there was little to be had in England or continental Europe, where much of the potato and grain harvest had failed in 1846. To help alleviate hunger in their own countries European governments passed laws against the export of food. Orders were sent to purchase more Indian corn (maize) from the United States, but it was too late: other European nations had bought up all the available corn, and order for the next summer's harvest already exceeded the anticipated crop. Some Protestants believed that the Irish famine was a message from God condemning the Irish way of life, particularly Catholicism. And many British political leaders were unwilling to support direct relief efforts, feeling that the Scottish and English Protestant working classes should not have to feed Irish Catholics.

Despite the failure of the potato harvest, Ireland was still a rich agricultural country that had exported food for decades. Potatoes were only 20 per cent of the total agricultural production of Ireland, and grain production exceeded that of potatoes. Much of Irish agriculture, however, was controlled by merchants who made more money from exporting food than by using their stores to feed the hungry in Ireland. Rather than outlawing the sale of food abroad, as other European governments had done, the Whig government permitted Irish products to be sold at the highest prices. During that fateful winter of 1846–7, more food was exported from Ireland to England than arrived in Ireland in the form of relief supplies.

In August 1846 the Whig government decreed that the landlords in Ireland should pay rates (taxes) for local relief efforts. Those resident landlords who were financially well-off played an active role in relief, but many landlords were verging on bankruptcy. Without more government support, they were unable to carry out relief efforts or fund the public works projects. To avoid bankruptcy, many landlords forcibly expelled tenants who did not pay their rents, with the evictions usually carried out by police and troops. This shifted the burden of relief from the landlords to the state, but the government was unable to provide for this massive number of homeless, penniless people. An estimated 400,000

Irish tenants were evicted. With no food or shelter, eviction was a death sentence. By September of 1846 newspapers began to report deaths due to starvation. The first to die were evicted squatters and children. Weakened by starvation, thousands of Irish died of contagious diseases – fever, jaundice, dysentery, scurvy, typhus and infections. The hospitals and workhouses were completely overrun and overwhelmed. During the winter an estimated 400,000 people died as a result of the famine, either directly from starvation or from exposure, exhaustion or related diseases.

Soup Kitchens

By January 1847 the Whig government recognized that its approach to relief had failed; as a last resort, soup kitchens were set up to feed the poor and destitute. These typically served about forty gallons (180 litres) of soup to some 200 people daily – clearly just a drop in the bucket in light of what was needed. When the potato blight had first struck in England, French-born Alexis Soyer, chef at London's Reform Club, had raised private funds to establish a soup kitchen. Soyer now proposed an even more efficient operation that could feed many more people. In January 1847 the British government invited him to construct a prototype soup kitchen, and Soyer opened the facility in Dublin in April. In a temporary shelter built of canvas and wood stood a steam boiler with a 300-gallon (1,365-litre) capacity and an oven for baking bread. Once the soup was cooked, it was poured into thousand-gallon double-boilers called *bain-maries*, to keep it warm before serving. At serving time, a bell was rung, and the first hundred people were ushered in through the front door. Soup bowls were distributed and filled. As soon as everyone was seated, grace was said, and soup consumption commenced. Precisely six minutes later the bell rang again, and the first group filed out of the back door as another shift came in the front. Soyer's kitchen fed eight thousand people each day during the first few months. At the height of the famine, 26,000 people passed through daily. The soup kitchen was so successful that the British government bought it and handed over its operation to the Relief Committee. Other soup kitchens opened, following Soyer's model, and by May of 1847 800,000 people were being fed in these facilities. Three months later, the total hit three million.

Food poured in from America and additional deaths from starvation were averted. In the summer of 1847 the Irish crops looked promising, so the government declared the famine over and closed down relief operations on 15 August 1847. While the 1847–8 harvest was better than the previous year's, it didn't provide quite enough food to sustain the Irish population through the winter. The summer of 1848 was

Rotting potatoes hit by blight, such as those depicted in this sketch of 1846, made desperate the situation of many small tenants like Tom Sullivan of County Kerry, here examining his ruined crop.

unseasonably cold, and once again the potato crop failed completely; hundreds of thousands of Irish perished, while those who could emigrated elsewhere. The potato blight continued to destroy the crops for the next two years, although the severity of the disaster was somewhat lessened. But between 1849 and 1852 another 250,000 Irish were evicted from their homes.

A few landlords with funds supported those who were willing to emigrate, and many Irish sought new homes in England. Beginning in April 1847, an estimated 85,000 Irish departed for North America. Ships that had been used to transport pitch and other naval stores from Canada to the United Kingdom were pressed into service; these slow-moving freighters lacked amenities for passengers, who were required to provide their own food, bedding, and medical assistance. Since many of the immigrants were already weakened by the famine, and some were ill, about 20 per cent died on the long voyage across the Atlantic. When the survivors arrived in Canada or the United States, they found that their problems were just beginning. Poor, weak, sick, the immigrants were largely unskilled and unprepared for the demands of the urban workplace. Previous Irish immigrants, who had moved to North America prior to 1845, were mainly small farmers of Scottish Presbyterian descent, and they were unwilling to assist the new flood of Catholics.

The Effects of the Potato Famine

The potato famine ended in 1851. In England, Scotland, Continental Europe and North America it continued to affect specific populations for a few years afterwards. As there was no known way to stop the blight, many potato farmers just shifted to growing other crops. By the mid-1850s farmers had discovered that some varieties were more resistant to the blight, and potato-growing re-emerged as the world's most important vegetable in bulk and value.

The effects of the famine in Ireland were very different. By 1851 more than a million Irish, mainly from the western part of the country, had died due to hunger or disease exacerbated by malnutrition. Tens of thousands of Irish emigrated to England and Wales, where riots broke out against them. An additional million immigrants fled Ireland for North America, of whom 84 per cent ended up in the United States, where they faced prejudice and poverty for decades. Nevertheless, these new Americans encouraged those still living in Ireland to join them in the 'land of plenty'. As the economic conditions in Ireland did not dramatically improve after the famine, during the next fifty years another four million Irish left the country, coming mainly to North America. By 1900 the population of Ireland was just four million – half the number that had lived there in 1841. This vast migration not only changed Irish society, but also indelibly changed the countries where Irish immigrants settled.

Of those who survived the famine and remained in Ireland, many were scarred for life. A large number of surviving Irish died early due to suffering illnesses and mental disorders that were related to their experience of the famine. The Potato Famine was a defining event in the history of modern Ireland. It was immortalized in Irish songs, such as 'Dear Old Skibbereen', in which an immigrant tells his son of his travails during the famine; the son promises to return to Skibbereen to wreak vengeance on the British government. Many Irish concluded that famine had not been inevitable, as there had been enough food in Ireland to feed everyone, but that the British simply didn't care about the deaths of hundreds of thousands of Catholics.

Two young women setting seeds in lazy beds and breaking clods with their spades, Glenshesk, Co. Antrim, *c.* 1900.

While it took almost seventy years for the Irish to gain enough strength to revolt against England, they did so when England was facing the worst moments of the First World War. While most of Ireland gained independence in 1921, Northern Ireland remained part of the United Kingdom, and has remained a flashpoint ever since. When the Second World War came along Ireland remained neutral, and closed its ports to Allied ships. The large number of Irish immigrants in the US contributed to the isolationism that kept America out of the First World War until 1917, and out of the Second World War until December 1941, when the attack on Pearl Harbor made engagement inevitable.

The cause of the blight was little understood in the mid-nineteenth century, despite extensive efforts to find out what had caused it. Some thought it was the unusually wet weather; others blamed bad soil. Still others, particularly Protestant evangelicals, proclaimed that God was punishing Catholics in Ireland. One observer, Rev. M. J. Berkeley in Northhamptonshire, England, concluded that the blight was caused by a fungus, which was visible on the leaves of infected plants, and he published his findings in January 1846.

Controversy ensued, and it was not until after Louis Pasteur's groundbreaking work on microbes that scientists concluded that the culprit was indeed a fungus-like organism called *Phytophthora infestans*. Austin Bourke, author of a late-nineteenth-century book on the potato famine, concluded that the fungus had originated in the humid forests of central Mexico and then spread to cultivated potatoes in the late 1830s. The blight might well have remained a localized problem, but air currents spread the fungus from Mexico to the United States in the early 1840s. It was then inadvertently shipped to Belgium on infected seed potatoes in 1843.

Recent DNA research, however, has called this trajectory into question. In the 1990s Dr Jean Ristaino, a plant pathologist at North Carolina State University, examined potato plant leaves from the nineteenth and twentieth centuries and concluded that the fungus most likely originated in South America, not Mexico. In the 1840s ships regularly transported potatoes as a food source for the crew, which likely contributed to the spread of the pathogen to Europe and the United States.

The potato blight remains alive and well in Europe and North America. Every year millions of tons of potatoes are lost to its ravages, and in years that are particularly wet the loss is much greater.

4
The Culinary Potato

For 400 years, the potato has filled the bellies of hungry people the world over and pleased the palates of connoisseurs. The popularity of the potato rests on its versatility: it can be boiled, fried, sliced, diced, mashed, scalloped and baked. It can be a component in pancakes, salads, soups, puddings and chowders. It complements virtually any poultry, meat or fish. As it is cheap and relatively easy to grow, it is available to rich and poor alike. This chapter will examine the diverse ways the potato is eaten, and how it reached its culinary apogee in the mid-nineteenth century.

The indigenous people of South America ate potatoes, a dietary staple, in a variety of ways: they boiled, roasted or baked them, and most likely made potatoes into gruels or bread-like products. When the potato arrived in Europe, it found a place in established eating habits and culinary styles. According to the German historian Günter Wiegelmann, the first European potato recipe appeared in a 1581 letter, which encouraged the Elector of Saxony, Christian 1, to boil potatoes and cook them in butter. Several recipes for *Erdtepffel* ('earth apple') appear in Marx Rumpolt's cookbook *Ein new Kochbuch* (A New Cookbook), first published in Germany in 1581. Rumpolt was in the employ of the Elector of Mainz,

and his work was filled with more than two thousand sophis-
ticated recipes reflecting the highest standard of German
cookery. Some historians claim that this book contains the
first European recipe for potatoes; Wiegelmann maintains
that the 'Erdtepffel' Rumpolt referred to was the round fruit
of a member of the cucurbitaceae family. A recipe calling for
onions and grated 'earth apples' appears in Anna Weckerin's
Ein köstlich new Köchbuch (A Delicious New Cookbook), first
published in Bavaria in 1597. Weckerin's father and husband
were both professors who taught medicine, and she was one
of the first women to publish a cookbook. Some have claimed
that her book contains a recipe for potato cakes, but again,
the ingredient she called for is not likely the potato. Whatever
vegetable Rumpolt and Weckerin intended for their recipes,
it is a fact that potatoes were grown in Germany in the late
sixteenth century, and a number of modern culinary historians have successfully prepared Rumpolt's and Weckerin's
recipes using potatoes.

John Gerard states in his *Herball* (1597) that potatoes can
be 'either rosted [sic] in the embers, or boyled and eaten with
oyle, vinegar, and pepper, or dressed any other way by the
hand of some cunning in cookerie'. A number of recipes for
potatoes appeared in a book by John Forster, published in
1664. *Englands Happiness Increased* offers the following: 'How
to make Paste of Potatoes' (including recipes for pies, pastries,
and tarts); 'How to make Puddings of Potatoes' (including
both baked and boiled puddings); 'How to make very good
Custards of Potatoes'; 'How to make Potato Cheesecakes';
and 'To Make Cakes of Potatoes'. Potato pies were among the
more common recipes in cookbooks, although many such
recipes referred to sweet potatoes rather than white potatoes.
The anonymously written *True Gentleman's Delight* (1676) supplies this recipe for an exceedingly rich potato pie:

A Potato-Pye for Supper

Take three pound of boiled and blanched potatoes, and three nutmegs, and half an ounce of cinnamon beaten together, and three ounces of sugar, season your potatoes, and put them in your pie, then take the marrow of three bones rouled in yolks of eggs, and sliced lemon and large mace, and half a pound of butter, six dates quartered, put this into your pie, and let it stand an hour in the oven, then make a sharp caudle of butter, sugar, verjuice and white-wine, put it in when you take your pie out of the oven.[2]

William Salmon, author of *The Family Dictionary, or Household Companion* of 1695, expounded upon the culinary and medicinal uses of potatoes:

The preparations of the potato are: (1) boiled, baked or roasted roots, (2) the broth ... *The Prepared Roots:* They stop fluxes of the bowels, nourish much, and restore in a pining consumption; being boiled, baked or roasted, they are eaten with good butter, salt, juice of oranges or lemons, and double refined sugar, as common food: they increase seed and provoke lust, causing fruitfulness in both sexes: and stop all sorts of fluxes of the belly. *The Broth of the Roots:* They are first boiled soft in fair water, then taken out and peeled, afterwards put into the same water again, and boiled till the broth becomes as thick, as very thick cream, or thin Hasty Pudding: some mix an equal quantity of milk with it, and so make broth; others after they are peeled, instead of putting them into the waters they were boiled in, boil them only in milk, till they are dissolved as aforesaid, and the broth is made pleasant with sweet butter, a little salt and double refined sugar, and so eaten.[3]

Thomas Houghton, author of *The Golden Treasury* (1699), wrote that in Great Britain potatoes were boiled or roasted, and eaten with butter and sugar. By the mid-eighteenth century potato recipes were published in profusion in England. Dozens of potato recipes, for instance, appear in Richard Bradley's 'Discourse Concerning the Improvement of the Potato' (1732) and William Ellis's *The Modern Husbandman* (1744).

In Germany potato recipes began to appear in the mid-seventeenth century. A gardener's journal dated 1648 includes a recipe for boiling potatoes, removing their skins, boiling them again with wine, butter and spices, and serving them with ginger sprinkled on top. Sigismund Elsholtz's *Diaeteticon* (1682) notes that potatoes were commonly grown in Germany. The *Frauenzimmerlexikon* (1715) includes four potato recipes,

Baked potato with butter, one of the most common ways to serve potatoes in Europe and America.

including ones for soups and salads.⁴ After 1750 recipes for potatoes were found in virtually all German cookbooks.

Benjamin Thompson, a Massachusetts-born supporter of the British during the American War for Independence, moved to Bavaria in 1791, where he worked to develop economical ways to feed the poor. Many of his recipes contained potatoes, and these were widely used throughout Europe for public relief for the poor. For his work, he was honored with the title of 'Graf von Rumford'. His 'Essay of Food and Particularly on Feeding the Poor', published in 1796, included dozens of recipes, many German in origin, that included potatoes.⁵

Potato Salad

Potato salads are a feature of many different cuisines, including German, Dutch, French, Indian and American. They are particularly associated with regional German cuisine. Called a 'salad' because it consists of vegetables coated with dressing, it is more usually served as a side dish. Southern German potato salads are often served warm or hot, dressed with a vinegar sauce prepared in a skillet in which bacon has been cooked, while others are served at room temperature. In the United States and northern Germany chilled potato salads are favoured. In the US cubed potatoes are usually dressed with mayonnaise; chopped hard-boiled eggs, celery, onion and herbs are common additions. Potato salad is one of the quintessential items on the American picnic menu.

Here is Count Rumford's late eighteenth-century recipe for a refined potato salad, which actually sounds more French than German:

A dish in high repute in some parts of Germany, and which deserves to be particularly recommended, is a salad of potatoes. The potatoes being properly boiled and skinned are cut into thin slices, and the same sauce which is commonly used for salads of lettuce is poured over them. Some mix anchovies with this sauce, which gives it a very agreeable relish, and with potatoes it is remarkably palatable.[6]

Fritters, Pancakes, Latkes, Hash Browns, Home Fries and Rösti

The indigenous peoples of South America invented many techniques for preparing potatoes, but frying wasn't one of them. Frying as a cooking method developed in the Old World, and was not employed in the New World until after the arrival of Europeans. The prevalence of frying was hindered in the New World by the absence of an obvious frying medium, such as lard or olive oil, and the lack of metal pans that could withstand the high temperatures required in frying. In Europe, however, frying – in deep or shallow fat – has been a common mode of preparing potatoes since the sixteenth century, and a wide variety of fried potato dishes emerged in Europe and the Americas in the ensuing centuries.

Fritters or pancakes may be made of either cooked, mashed potatoes or grated raw potatoes, sometimes bound with eggs and breadcrumbs and seasoned with onions and herbs. They had became a common food by the eighteenth century. Ideally, they are moist on the inside, with a crisp crust. Here is Richard Bradley's eighteenth-century recipe for potato fritters:

Take of the Potato-Pulp mash'd and strain'd from its Juices, after the Potatoes have been carefully boil'd, mix them with Milk, Powder of Cloves, Cinnamon, and double refin'd Loaf-Sugar, of each enough to render the Batter palatable; then, shred some Apples small, and mix them well with the Batter, and fry them like other Fritters in Hog's Lard.[7]

Bradley recommends garnishing the fritters with sugar and orange slices.

Potato pancakes are found in Irish, Jewish, Polish, German, Ukrainian, Czech, Belarusian, Russian, Spanish, Ecuadorian, Indian and Korean cookery. They are served with a variety of accompaniments, such as cheese, peanut sauce, sour cream, jam or applesauce. Potato pancakes have various names, including *deruny* or *draniki* in the Ukraine, Belorussia and Russia, and *Kartoffelpuffer* in Germany. *Latkes* are traditionally eaten by Jews during Hanukkah.

Similar to potato pancakes are hash-brown potatoes. This North American dish is made with diced, chopped or shredded cooked potatoes (sometimes accented with onion or bell pepper), which are fried in a skillet or on a griddle, often in bacon grease. The cook presses the potatoes with a spatula to form them into a crisply browned cake. Hash browns are usually served for breakfast, with eggs and bacon.

Another breakfast favourite, cottage fries or home fries, can be made with either raw or cooked potatoes cut in slices. They're cooked in fat until browned but not crisp. If chopped onions and bell peppers are added, the dish is called Potatoes O'Brien. Lyonnaise potatoes, a somewhat more elegant dish usually served as a side dish at lunch or dinner, is composed of sautéed sliced potatoes and onions.

Rösti is the world-famous Swiss version of the potato cake; it has a golden crust and is tender and pale on the inside. Raw potatoes are cut into matchsticks and fried in butter

Sergey Prokudin-Gorsky, photograph of potato farming in Russian Empire, *c.* 1905–15.

until they form a 'mat' that can be flipped in the pan. Sometimes a little grated cheese is sprinkled on top after the cake is flipped over.

Chips and Fries, Part 1

The art of deep-frying was perfected in France during the late eighteenth century. Deep-fried potatoes took on a variety of shapes and names. By the late eighteenth century, deep-fried potato sticks or fingers were called *pommes de terre frites*, which was shortened to *pommes frites* (frequently pronounced and written *pomfrits*). The US President Thomas Jefferson, who had brought a French chef into the White

House when he became president in 1801, made a note of a recipe for '*Pommes de terre frites à cru, en petites tranches*' (raw potatoes cut into small strips and fried), which may well have reflected this tradition. As *pommes frites* became more common the name was further shortened to *frites*, and these were commonly served at fashionable dinners and restaurants throughout France and Belgium during the nineteenth and twentieth centuries. Today they are as ubiquitous in those countries – and many others in Europe – as French fries are in the US.

In the eighteenth and nineteenth centuries the culinary term *chips* was applied to small slices or chunks of vegetables and fruit, such as apricots, peaches, pineapples, pumpkins and potatoes. Most chips were made by drying or dehydrating the fruit or vegetable, but potato chips were fried. In England this 'chip' terminology became ingrained in 'fish and chips'. These were originally popularized by a newly arrived Jewish immigrant from Eastern Europe, Joseph Malin, who opened the first combined fish and chip shop in London in the 1860s. Today fish and chips are served in an estimated 8,000 chip shops, and the combination is considered Britain's national dish. Fish and chips are also popular throughout the former British Empire, in Australia, Canada, Ireland, New Zealand and South Africa.

The term 'French fried potatoes' was used by the British cookbook author Eliza Warren, whose *Cookery Works for All Maids* (1856) includes a recipe for fried potatoes cut into long strips. Warren's cookbook, with her 'French fried Potatoes' recipe, was published in the United States in 1858, and the recipe was picked up in turn by American cookbook writers. A typical method for 'French Fried Potatoes' appears in the first edition of Fannie Farmer's popular *Boston Cooking-School Cook Book* (1896):

Wash and pare small potatoes, cut in eighths length-wise, and soak one hour in cold water. Take from water, dry between towels, and fry in deep fat. Drain on brown paper and sprinkle with salt.

Care must be taken that fat is not too hot, as potatoes must be cooked as well as browned.

But there were other names as well, including 'German fried potatoes' and 'German fries'. During the First World War German place names – such as New Berlin, Ohio, now called New Canton – and the word 'German' were expunged from the American language, and by 1918 'French fries', shortened to 'fries', had won the name game in the United States and Canada. American soldiers disseminated the term throughout the Pacific during the Second World War, and it is commonly used in New Zealand and Australia. Today, throughout the former Empire, 'fries' is used interchangeably with 'chips', although 'chips' is far more common in Britain.

Potato products being manufactured at the new Lutosa Industries factory, Leuze en Hainaut, Belgium, 2004.

During the twentieth century, fries became popular throughout the world under a variety of names. They are served with diverse condiments and foods. For instance, steamed mussels and fries (*mosselen-friet* or *moules-frites*), are popular in Belgium. In France, steak and fries (*steak-frites*) is a bistro mainstay. Fried eggs with fries (*huevos con patatas*) is a popular meal in Spain. Poutine (fries with gravy and cheese) is a beloved 'comfort' food in Québéc.

Mashed Potatoes

Mashed potatoes are made by mashing boiled or baked potatoes with a ricer, masher or fork. The potatoes may be peeled either before or after cooking, and, during the mashing, enriched with butter, cream, cheese, sour cream, milk or eggs, and seasoned with salt, pepper, garlic, bacon bits, spices and herbs. Recipes for mashed potatoes appeared in the mid-eighteenth century. Hannah Glasse's recipe in *The Art of Cookery* (1747) is relatively simple: 'Boil your Potatoes, peel them, and . . . mash them well; To two Pounds of Potatoes put a Pint of Milk . . . stir in, and serve it up.'

Many types and configurations of potato mashers were patented in the United States during the mid-nineteenth century, including potato ricers – lever-operated presses with a perforated plate through which the potato was extruded – which became popular at the end of the century. Dehydrated and frozen mashed potatoes became commercially available in the middle of the twentieth century.

Mashed potatoes serve as the basis for other dishes, including potato croquettes and potato pancakes. Duchess potatoes or *Pommes duchesse* were a French invention of the late nineteenth century in which mashed potatoes are enriched with eggs and cream and then piped through a pastry tube in decorative shapes, such as ribbons and rosettes, and baked until browned.

Potato Dumplings

A wide variety of dumplings have been made from potato dough or stuffed with potato fillings. Dumplings may be boiled or baked, and some are fried just before serving. In Slavic countries, *pierogies*, small semi-circular dumplings made with a simple flour dough, often contain a potato filling. Swedish potato dumplings, *Palt*, or *Pitepalt*, are often filled with bits of salt pork. The Italian pasta dumplings called *gnocchi* have been

Mashed, one of the most common ways of serving potatoes in Europe and America.

around since ancient Roman times, and since the seventeenth century they have commonly been made from potatoes.

Potato dumplings are traditional in many parts of Germany. In the state of Thüringia, dumplings made from a combination of raw or boiled potatoes are so celebrated that the city of Heichelheim has established a museum, the Thüringer Klossmuseum, to honour them.

The American-born Count Rumford, who worked in Bavaria to find ways to feed the poor, offered advice on many uses of the potato. Here is his recipe:

Recipe for a very cheap Potato-Dumplin

Take any quantity of potatoes, half boiled; skin or pare them, and grate them to a coarse powder with a grater; mix them up with a very small quantity of flour, $^{1}/_{16}$, for instance, of the weight of the potatoes, or even less; add a seasoning of salt, pepper, and sweet herbs; mix up the whole with boiling water to a proper consistency, and form the mass into dumplins of the size of a large apple. Roll the dumplins, when formed, in flour, to prevent the water from penetrating them, and put them into boiling water, and boil them till they rise to the surface of the water, and swim, when they will be found to be sufficiently done.

These dumplins may be made very savoury by mixing with them a small quantity of grated hung beef, or of pounded red herring.

Fried bread may likewise be mixed with them, and this without any other addition, except a seasoning of salt, forms an excellent dish.[8]

Soups, Stews and Chowders

Gruels, soups, stews and chowders were among the first culinary uses of the potato in Europe. Beginning in the late seventeenth century, many cookbooks include recipes for soups and stews made with potatoes. Potato soups were particularly popular in Germany.

The word *chowder* comes from the French *chaudière*, a type of kettle, and fishermen along the coast of France originated these simple seafood stews. The ingredients vary from place to place and from season to season, but fish or shellfish and potatoes are fairly constant components. This often created a thick, highly seasoned dish without cooking the ingredients down to a mush. Chowders migrated to England, where they became a speciality of Cornish fishermen. With English colonists, chowder crossed the Atlantic Ocean to Newfoundland and New England, and recipes were published in British cookbooks beginning in the mid-eighteenth century.

Thomas F. DeVoe, the American author of *The Market Assistant* (1867), put forward a traditional fish chowder recipe made with cod and potatoes:

> Fish-chowder.
> Take a codfish about six or seven pounds, cut in slices about one inch thick; take six or seven medium-sized potatoes and cut in slices; take one pound salt pork, cut in slices, and fried brown; when sufficiently done, take out the pork from the pot with one half the fat. Now put in a layer of fish, then some of the potatoes and pork, with some pilot-bread; and so on, alternately, until all is in the pot. Pour over the whole quart of water and one pint of milk; add salt and pepper to your taste, and boil twenty minutes. A few onions improve it for those who are fond of them.

Potato soups have continued to evolve. The chilled leek-and-potato purée called *vichyssoise* was first served in 1917 by Louis Diat, chef at the Hotel Ritz-Carlton in New York City. Although Diat may not have invented the soup, he was the first to brand it '*vichyssoise*', and that is what Americans still call it.

Because they are cheap, filling and nutritious, potato soups have been found useful in feeding the poor and starving. Here is Count Rumford's recipe for a plain but sustaining dish to be served at soup kitchens:

> The water and the pearl barley are first put together into the boiler and made to boil; the pease are then added, and the boiling is continued over a gentle fire about two hours; the potatoes are then added, (having been previously peeled with a knife, or having been boiled, in order to their being more easily deprived of their skins,) and the boiling is continued for about one hour more, during which time the contents of the boiler are frequently stirred about with a large wooden spoon, or ladle, in order to destroy the texture of the potatoes, and to reduce the soup to one uniform mass. When this is done, the vinegar and the salt are added; and last of all, at the moment it is to be served up, the cuttings of bread.[9]

In the eighteenth century, Irish stew was traditionally made of mutton (usually neck), potatoes, onions and parsley, although some cooks added turnips or parsnips, carrots and barley. Mutton was the dominant ingredient because of the economic importance of wool and sheep's milk in Ireland: only old sheep ended up in the stew pot, where it needed hours of simmering before it was palatable. When made in the traditional manner, even with tender lamb, Irish stew is cooked long enough that the vegetables break down, and the result is a very thick and hearty stew. It was recognized as the Irish national dish about 1800.

In the United States, N.K.M. Lee's *The Cook's Own Book* (1832) includes a recipe for Irish stew that is made from the same ingredients and in the same way as in Ireland. However, in America lamb and mutton were not plentiful, so other meats were substituted. Today, lamb is once again the meat most often used in Irish stew.

Potato Bread and Cake

It did not take potato growers long to find a way to make flour from potatoes, and the next step was to add this to wheat or rye flour to make bread. Beginning in the early eighteenth century, references to potato bread were published. Initially potato flour was probably used because it was cheaper than wheat or rye flour, especially in times of famine or scarcity; but later some bakers concluded that adding potato flour – or mashed potatoes – produced a better-tasting bread. At any rate, potato flour alone will not make a satisfactory bread because it does not develop gluten, which is necessary to give the bread substance and shape. A 1744 recipe for potato bread is very simple:

> This Root has often been employed, like the Turnep, towards making Loaves of Bread in the scarce Times of Corn. Take as much boiled Pulp of Potatoes, as Wheaten Flour, Weight for Weight, and knead them together as common Dough is done for Bread.[10]

In Germany potato bread may contain spelt and rye flour. In Ireland pratie oaten is made with mashed potatoes and rolled

Clockwise from top left: *Tu dou si*; Moroccan tagine; homemade *papas con chorizo*; *Nikujaga*, a Japanese beef and potato stew.

oats. In Scotland tattie scones are made from mashed potatoes and just enough flour to make a dough that can be rolled and cut, and in England recipes for potato cakes frequently appeared in the nineteenth century.

Modern Potato Recipes

There are of course thousands of different potato dishes around the world. In Japan *nikujaga*, a meat and potato stew, is one of the most popular potato dishes. There are many

Middle Eastern potato recipes, such as Moroccan braises (potatoes with saffron, lemon and olives). The Spanish *tortilla de patatas* is a thick, skillet-cooked cake of fried, sliced potatoes held together with beaten egg. One of the most popular Spanish tapas is *patatas bravas*, cubes of sautéed potato served with a hot and tangy sauce. In Mexico *papas con chorizo* (diced potatoes cooked with hot sausage) are served with toast or tortillas, for breakfast. In China *tu dou si* is a savoury dish of julienned or sliced potatoes stir-fried with various accompaniments such as peppers, garlic and ginger; and in Canada, potato scallop, consisting of thinly sliced potatoes, onions, breadcrumbs, milk and other ingredients, is a traditional dish.

5
The Commercial Potato

As potatoes are so easily grown and the plants are so prolific, potatoes are usually cheap. As a result, many food products and even a few beverages are made from them. Historically, the majority of potatoes grown in the world were baked and boiled before use, and many potato varieties were developed for this purpose. In North America, for instance, Russet potatoes, which have a low moisture content and high starch, are the main variety used for baking, while Round White potatoes, which have a higher moisture content and lower starch, are firmer and are usually used for boiling. In the United Kingdom, Marfona and Vivaldi are usually baked, while the best boiling potatoes are the Harmony and Osprey. The Estima variety are used for both boiling and baking.

Today, the majority of potatoes grown in the world are used for commercial purposes other than baking or boiling. The more commercial common products in the nineteenth century were potato starch and flour, potato yeast, potato sugar, potato schnapps and, last but not least, vodka. As the prices of other commodities, such as wheat and sugarcane, declined during the late nineteenth century, potato products became less common, but some are still manufactured today. Potato starch or potato flour is used as an alternative to wheat

Russet Burbank, the most important commercial potato variety today.

Royales de Jersey potatoes. Jersey Royal potatoes are grown only on the island of Jersey off the coast of Normandy, France.

A variety of potatoes being sold in the marketplace.

flour for thickening in sauces and soups. Cakes baked during Passover, when wheat flour may not be used, are sometimes made with potato flour, which also turns up in bread recipes. Because it is gluten-free, potato flour is a boon to those who are allergic to gluten. Potato starch is increasingly being used in many food-industry applications, such as making gum confections, food flavourings and thickeners, as well as in animal feed, medicine, chemicals, paper-making, architecture and oil extraction.

Luther Burbank

In the mid-nineteenth century, potatoes were relatively small, unattractive and not of uniform size. In 1872 Luther Burbank, an amateur gardener in Lunenburg, Massachusetts, found a seedball (the fruit produced by the potato with seeds

Fresh potatoes for sale – white, red and new varieties for sale at Ottawa's Byward Market.

for reproduction) growing on the stem of an 'Early Rose' potato in his garden. It was unusual for the Early Rose to produce a seedball, and Burbank wondered what novelties might sprout if he planted the seeds. All 23 seeds matured, and all the plants produced potatoes of different shapes, sizes and colours. One very productive plant yielded large white

Root potatoes in a burlap sack, including organic fingerling potatoes, red, white, purple and sweet potatoes.

tubers with brown skins. Burbank nurtured these potatoes, and in 1875 he convinced a seedsman to buy the rights to them. Burbank sold his farm and moved to Santa Rosa, in northern California, where he began a massive campaign to improve the fruits and vegetables grown there.

In 1914 a Colorado farmer found that some of his Burbank potatoes had reddish-brown skins, and from these he produced the potato variety called the Russet Burbank. The variety was slow to catch on – only 4 per cent of the potatoes grown in the United States in 1930 were Russet Burbanks. But the potatoes were good for the fresh market, and growers in Idaho began to cultivate them; still, sales were limited.

Of course, the Russet Burbank was just one potato variety. The *World Catalogue of Potato Varieties* lists more than 4,500, which fall into five broad categories based largely on skin colour: blue-/purple-skinned, pink-/red-skinned, russet-skinned, white-/tan-skinned and yellow-skinned. The propagation of potatoes is big business today, and it will likely be even bigger business in the future as genetically modified potatoes become an important addition to the commercial potato crop.

Chips and Fries, Part II

Beginning in the early twentieth century, potato fries were occasionally served in American cafes, diners and roadside eateries, but this delectable finger food required considerable effort to prepare. The cook had to peel and cut the potatoes according to demand; left uncooked, cut potato sticks would turn grey. The frying fat (usually lard) had to be kept at a constant temperature of 340–70°F (170–88°C); if too many potatoes were dropped into the fryer at once, the fat would cool down, resulting in flabby, greasy fries. French fries must be served fresh and hot, or they quickly turn soggy and limp. Employees had to be trained to meet these exacting standards, a time-consuming process. And working around a vat of boiling hot fat could lead to disastrous accidents – a fact that convinced many restaurant managers that French fries just weren't worth the trouble.

During the Second World War meat was rationed and became scarce in the United States. Cafes, diners, snack bars and roadside stands had to serve something to round out their downsized or unavailable burgers. Potatoes remained plentiful and cheap, and they were never rationed. During the war French fries became a staple on many restaurant menus around the nation. By the time that rationing ended after the war, Americans had taken a liking to french fries and their sales increased. However, some restaurant chains, such as White Castle, stopped serving them because the deep-frying set-up posed a danger to their workers. However, during the

French fries being manufactured at the official opening of Lutosa Industries' new frozen food factory, Leuze en Hainaut, Belgium, 2004.

1950s safer fryers came on the market, and French fries became a fixture in the fast-food industry.

French fries, which are more profitable than hamburgers, were a flagship item at the fledgling McDonald's restaurant chain. The founders of the chain, Richard and Maurice McDonald, believed that French fries were one of the most important factors in their success. They perfected the frying process and promoted the relationship between hamburgers and fries. The brothers used Russet Burbank potatoes, which were peeled daily and cut into very thin sticks, and cooked them in special fryers that turned out very crisp fries. As the chain began to expand in the 1960s, McDonald's contracted with dozens of different growers for their potatoes, and the uniformity of the fries declined. Ray Kroc, who acquired McDonald's from the brothers in 1961, began looking for better ways to prepare and distribute French fries to his franchises.

French fries had been commercially frozen since 1946, but most home cooks didn't want to be bothered with deep frying, and the potatoes' flavour was lacklustre. In 1953 Idaho potato-grower J. R. Simplot started producing frozen French fries, and four years later a Canadian firm, McCain Foods Ltd, began making them. The new product eliminated the tasks of peeling and cutting, but the potatoes still had to be deep fried, which deterred home cooks. There was little interest from restaurants, either, because of the accidents and fires that deep fryers often caused.

Simplot concluded that the real market for his frozen fries was the booming fast-food business, and he sought out chains that might be interested in the labour-saving benefits of frozen fries. Simplot met Ray Kroc in 1965, and the French-fry world was changed forever. Working with the Simplot potato company, McDonald's researchers devised ways of freezing raw fries and retaining their flavour and texture. For optimal flavour, McDonald's and many other fast-food chains filled their fryers with a mixture of 7 per cent soy oil and 93 per cent beef tallow.

As American fast-food establishments began to spread around the world, the term 'fries' became common in most countries, including those English-speaking countries which traditionally used the word 'chips'. In these countries, the obvious exception was the continued use of the phrase 'fish and chips'.

A small cult of condiments has built up around French fries and chips. Salt is a universal, but other condiments vary with the locale: ketchup is king in the United States, while malt vinegar and tartare sauce are common when chips are served with fish in Great Britain. Mayonnaise is the topping of choice in Belgium, and Indonesian-style saté sauce is popular in the Netherlands. English-speaking Canadians sprinkle their fries with white vinegar, while in Québec fries are served topped with cheese curds and brown gravy, a dish called *poutine*. A grated white brine cheese, called *sirene*, is commonly served on fries in Bulgaria; in Poland, a garlic sauce is preferred. Filipinos like their fries with a cheese sauce, while sugar and butter are preferred in Vietnam. Wattie's tomato sauce (a brand of ketchup) is a necessity in New Zealand.

Frying Problems

In 1989, when it was revealed that McDonald's used beef tallow in making their French fries, vegetarians were outraged that the company had not informed customers of this. Meanwhile, nutrition watchdogs protested the amount of cholesterol in the fries. In 1990, with considerable fanfare, McDonald's announced a switch to vegetable oil with 'added natural flavorings'. When it was disclosed that those flavourings included beef tallow, Hindu customers in India ransacked a Bombay McDonald's and smeared cow dung on a statue of Ronald McDonald. (The company denied that any beef product had ever been used in its restaurants in India.) In the United States twelve vegetarians sued McDonald's for falsely stating that the fries were vegetarian, a claim that the company denied making. McDonald's eventually settled out of court, agreeing to post an apology on the company's website, and to give $10 million to vegetarian organizations and pay off the twelve individuals involved in the suit.

McDonald's continued to innovate in the way its French fries were prepared. It was the first fast-food company to employ computers to automatically adjust cooking times and temperatures. It created a rapid frying system for frozen potatoes that cut cooking time by 30 to 40 seconds; when millions of customers order fries, the time saved easily covers the cost of the equipment. Eric Schlosser, author of *Fast-Food Nation,* has pointed out that the special taste of McDonald's French fries does not derive from the type of potatoes, the technology used in processing them or the machines that fry them; other chains buy from the same sources and use similar equipment. What gives McDonald's fries their unique taste is the chemical flavourings added to the oil.

During the past fifty years, the size of a portion of fast-food fries has steadily increased. Initially, McDonald's only offered a 'large' 2-ounce (57 g) size. In the 1970s, a 'small' order of fries was 2 oz, and the new 'large' weighed in at 6 oz (170 g). Then McDonald's 'supersized' a large portion of fries to 8 oz (227 g). Due to pressure (aroused, to some extent, by the documentary film *Super Size Me*, which purportedly documented the negative effects of eating supersized meals at McDonald's for thirty days) McDonald's discontinued this size, but other fast-food chains continue to serve 8-oz portions of fries.

Today, French fries are the single most popular fast food in America. As a result, annual sales of frozen French fries have grown dramatically over the past fifty years. In 1970 frozen French fries surpassed regular potato sales in the United States. By 2000 the production of frozen French fries worldwide grew to more than $1.9 billion. In 2004 Americans consumed 7.5 billion lb (3.4 billion kg) of frozen French fries, 90 per cent of which were sold by foodservice outlets.

A few fast-food outlets bucked the trend toward frozen fries and proudly tout their hand-cut fries. California's In-N-Out Burger chain uses Kennebec or Russet potatoes, depending on the season. The potatoes are cut by hand and soon afterward dropped in a deep fryer filled with cotton-seed oil. In-N-Out Burger offers regular French fries as well as 'Animal Fries', topped with cheese and grilled onions; 'Fries Well-Done' are cooked longer for a crisper texture. Five Guy's Hamburger and Fries, which was launched in the Washington, DC metro area, also uses fresh potatoes that are peeled and cut daily, and other small chains and restaurants around the country do the same.

As American fast-food chains moved abroad, so did production of frozen French fries. Russet Burbank potatoes are now grown in many countries today around the world. As of 2004, the United States remained the world's largest producer of frozen French fries; the Netherlands now ranks second, and Canada third.

Potato Chips or Crisps

By popular tradition, one George Crum, a cook at the Moon's Lake House in Saratoga, New York, was the first to fry thin potato slices into ultra-crisp chips, which came to be called Saratoga potatoes; these were served as an accompaniment to meat or game. In fact, though, recipes calling for fried 'shavings' of raw potatoes had appeared in American cookery books since 1824 – and thin 'Saratoga potatoes' were served with ice cream or sold in paper bags like confectionery at Moon's Lake House before Crum was employed there. Regardless of who invented them, recipes for 'Saratoga' potatoes and potato chips appeared regularly in American cookbooks beginning in the 1870s.

Potato chips were first mass-produced during the 1890s by a number of manufacturers, including John E. Marshall of Boston and William Tappendon of Cleveland, Ohio. They were sold in barrels to grocery stores. Proprietors dished out the chips into paper bags for customers, who warmed them

Potato crisps, known as 'chips' in the USA.

in the oven before serving. Unfortunately the chips were often stale, and the product never really caught on. The packaging problem was not solved until the 1930s, when potato chips were sold in vacuum-sealed bags. By that time, potato chips were a snack food rather than a side dish.

American-style potato chips began to be manufactured in Great Britain in the 1920s. To avoid confusion with 'chip potatoes', British manufacturers called their product 'potato crisps' or simply 'crisps'.

McCain products. Every day, the McCain factory in France produces 600 tons of frozen French fries.

Frito-Lay

In 1937 Herman W. Lay, an ambitious businessman from Nashville, Tennessee, bought Barrett Foods, a snack food company with plants in Atlanta and Memphis. The first product to bear the 'Lay's' brand name was popcorn; the company began manufacturing potato chips in 1938.

When the Second World War began, potato chips were initially declared a non-essential food in the United States, which meant that production would have to stop for the duration. Manufacturers lobbied the War Production Board

Cape Cod
Potato Chips.

to change this designation, and their efforts were successful. Potato chip sales increased throughout the war, in part because sugar and chocolate were rationed, limiting the availability of candy bars and other sweet snacks.

Herman Lay's firm had become a major regional producer of snack foods by the war's end. After the war, Lay automated his potato-chip manufacturing business and diversified its products. In 1945 he met Elmer Doolin, who manufactured Frito Corn Chips in San Antonio. Doolin franchized Herman Lay to distribute Fritos. The two companies cooperated on other products. In 1958 Lay acquired the rights from Frito-Lay to the new creation called 'Ruffles', a thick, 'corrugated' potato chip made especially for dipping.

In the 1960s Proctor & Gamble introduced Pringles, which are made from dehydrated and reconstituted potatoes. Unlike potato chips, Pringles are a uniform size and shape, making it possible to package Pringles in a long tube. The potato chip industry went to court to prevent Proctor & Gamble from calling Pringles 'potato chips'. It was resolved in 1975, when the US Food and Drug Administration defined Pringles as 'potato chips made from dehydrated potatoes'.

Americans purchase $6 billion of potato chips annually, which works out to about 17 lb (7.7 kg) of potato chips and shoestring potatoes per person. An additional $6 billion is spent on potato chips in other countries.

In 1994, following interviews with 100,000 people in 30 countries, PepsiCo decided to establish the potato chip as the world's most popular snack. They decided to increase sales and advertising in other countries using the Lay brand name. They built plants in foreign markets, conducted consumer research and created different flavours, such as shrimp for the Korean market and a squid-peanut flavour for Southeast Asia.

As American-style potato chips flooded the world market, the English word 'crisp' fell by the wayside in many countries, although 'Walker's Crisps' is the largest selling brand in England. New flavours emerged as indigenous manufacturers developed their own flavours. 'Tayto Crisps', for instance, an Irish brand sold in the United Kingdom, come in flavours such as Pickled Onion, Prawn Cocktail and Roast Chicken.

Other Potato Products

Historically, many vodkas were made from potatoes, but today most are made from grain or corn. However, from time to time, potato vodka has re-emerged.

During the First World War Germany used its abundance of potatoes to supplement the shortage of other food supplies. It tried making a variety of new products from potatoes. One was potato alcohol, which was also used as a substitute for petrol (gasoline). The mash derived as a waste-product in the manufacture of potato alcohol was used for animal feed. Today, potato alcohol has been offered as a solution for energy production.

Tater Tots, frozen, thimble-shaped nuggets of hash browns, were created in 1953 by Ore-Ida, as a means of utilizing potato shreds left over from French fry production. They first became available in stores in 1954. The American fast-food chain Sonic Drive-In features Tater Tots as a standard menu item, with cheese and/or chilli toppings. Burger King serves 'Cheesy Tots', which are thumb-shaped shredded potatoes with mozzarella and cheddar cheese inside. Various other names have been used for Tater Tots. Cascadian Farms has produced an organic version called Spud Puppies, and

Tacotime International has made Mexi-Fries (flavoured with Mexican-style spices or stuffed with cheese and diced jalapeno peppers) since the 1960s; the chain Taco Bell served similarly flavoured Mexi-Nuggets. Manufacturers outside the United States have produced similar products. Potato Gems, for instance, are sold in Australia, New Zealand and the United Kingdom, while Tasti Taters are produced by McCain Foods Limited in Canada.

Yet another product is dehydrated potato flakes, which are used to make a variety of foods. Invented by Canadian research scientist Edward A. Asselbergs in 1962, the flakes offer the advantages of a long storage period and convenient use in the home, by campers or in military field rations. The most common use is to make mashed potatoes, but they are also used to fabricate French fries and potato chips, such as Pringles. Dehydrated potatoes also fortify a wide range of processed snack foods, infant foods, baked breads, cakes and biscuits.

As grain prices have soared since 2002, it is extremely likely that potato products will continue to expand, especially in developing countries. The potato is versatile and inexpensive, and it will likely be commercially used in many different ways in the future.

The Unhealthy Potato

Although raw potatoes are filled with nutrition, its healthful components can be reduced in the cooking process and peeling greatly reduces their vitamin and fibre content. When they're cooked in water, vitamins will be lost unless the cooking water is incorporated in the finished dish (or saved for making soup). Deep frying or sautéing adds saturated fat and

Mexican poster stating the benefits of natural potatoes. The caption reads 'Compare antes de comprar papas' (Compare before buying potatoes).

cholesterol if they're cooked in bacon fat or butter. Even the exemplary nutritional profile of a baked potato can be compromised by drowning it in butter, gravy or sour cream.

Even when cooked in vegetable oil, commercial potato products have been criticized for their fat, trans-fat and salt content and their generally poor nutritional profile. This is seen as a particular problem for children and teenagers; approximately one-quarter of all vegetables consumed by American children are in the form of potato chips and French fries. In teenagers, the proportion increases to about one-third.

Commercial potato products are filled with calories and they often contain little nourishment. A large serving (169 g) of French fries, for instance, weighs in at 539 calories; just one ounce (28 g) of potato crisps or chips (about 10 chips) contains about 150 calories, and of course if dips are used they likely contain many more calories. One cup of mashed potatoes and butter has 237 calories, and if gravy or additional butter is added, calories increase further. Due to these high calories, many people have begun to eschew eating potatoes in virtually any form. To counteract these perceptions, potato companies have developed promotional programmes to point out the nutritional benefits of consuming potatoes. In a fascinating response, Western Potatoes in Australia has launched a marketing campaign with the publication of Joanne Beer's *The Potato Diet: Good Carbs Don't Make You Fat* (2008). Despite such efforts, in the past decade the consumption of potatoes has declined in North America and Europe.

6
The Cultural Potato

It addition to its historical, culinary and commercial significance, the potato has also starred in the cultural world in Europe and the Americas. Since ancient times, potato representations have appeared on sculptures and reliefs. From pre-Columbian America to the modern world, the potato has appeared in artistic works, plays, songs, games and politics.

The Artistic Potato

In ancient South America potato images were drawn on pottery. Depictions of potatoes have been found on pottery from the Nazca, Chimú and Moche civilizations on the northern coast of Peru. The Inca also produced depictions of potatoes on their pottery. Some pottery resembled potatoes, while others showed potatoes with human faces. The only known illustrations of the potato from Peru was included in a manuscript prepared by Huamán Poma (Don Felipe Huamán Pomade Ayala), a Peruvian chief who included four drawings of Inca planting and harvesting potatoes. The manuscript, written in the form of a letter to the King of Spain, went unpublished for almost three hundred years.

Pot, Proto-Chimu period, representing two twin tubers of *tunta*.

Pot, Inca period, made to look like a tuber of what was probably a cultivated variety, with a great number of 'eyes'.

Vincent Van Gogh, *The Potato Eaters*, 1885. This image illustrates the importance of potatoes in the diet of the poor peasants of Europe during the late nineteenth century.

Jean-François Millet, *Potato Planters*, c. 1861.

Joan Miró,
The Potato,
1928.

The first European illustration of the potato dates to 1589. The watercolour currently resides in the Plantin-Moretus Museum, Antwerp. Woodblock carvings were used to illustrate herbals, and John Gerard's *Herball* (1597) contains the earliest published depiction of the potato. For the next 200 years, potato plants and their tubers frequently appeared in herbals.

Beginning in the mid-nineteenth century, potatoes migrated into paintings, such as Daniel MacDonald's *The Discovery of Potato Blight* (*c.* 1852), Robert Warthmuller's *King in Potato Fields* (1896), William Merritt Chase's *The Potato Patch* (*c.* 1893), William Rothenstein's *Potato Planting* (1917), and Joan Miró's *The Potato* (1928). The term 'Potato Eaters' may initially have been a put-down aimed at the Irish, but the term shifted meaning after Vincent van Gogh's 1885 large-scale painting, *The Potato Eaters* ('De Aardappeleters'), became famous. Here unattractive Dutch peasants share their meagre potatoes at the end of the day.

Potato Slang

The word 'potato' has many slang meanings. For instance, in England calling something a 'potato' means it's a real, or proper thing. Conversely, saying something is 'not quite the clean potato' means that it's not completely sound or reliable. 'Small potatoes' is a humorous term applied to a person or event of little consequence, while 'rotten potatoes' has a very negative connotation. But in Australia, a *potater* is slang for a girl or woman. In the US 'potatoes' can also mean dollars, as in 'he's got 15,000 potatoes'.

A 'couch potato' – an expression that arose in the late twentieth century – is a person who spends most of their time slouching on the sofa, usually in front of the TV. More recently, the term 'mouse potato' was coined to describe someone who spends a great deal of time using a computer. Interestingly, this term was common in the nineteenth century, albeit with a totally different meaning: a dwarf potato plant.

The potato itself has acquired numerous different slang names, such as *spud*, which comes from the Irish word for spade. Others include *tattie* or *tatie*, a Scottish slang term, and 'Murphies', an Anglo-Irish-American slang term. *Poreens* or *pories* are Western Ireland terms meaning very small potatoes, and *chats* were small poor potatoes in England. The Anglo-Irish slang term for potatoes is *praties*, and *poundies* is an affectionate name for mashed potatoes. A Scottish dish that combines mashed potatoes and turnips is known as 'neeps and tatties'.

Advertisement for a 'Couch Potato' doll made by Coleco, USA, 1988.

By the late seventeenth century, the 'Irish potato' became a common phrase to distinguish white potatoes from sweet potatoes in England, and 'Irish "taters"' was used in America by 1745. 'Irishman's potato [sic] bowl', 'Irish potato rings' (dish rings, often made of silver) and 'Irish potato merchants' soon became part of the English language. There were also less neutral phrases. 'Potato eaters' and 'potato heads' became derogatory slang terms for the Irish, implying someone who was an unsophisticated, stupid, foolish hick. Likewise, *tattie howkers* was the pejorative term for Irish potato workers in Scotland.

The Playful Potato

Potatoes have become a part of the cultural lives of Americans and Europeans. The counting rhyme, 'One potato, Two potato', has been around at least since 1914. In 1942 'One Potato, Two Potato, Three Potato, Four' was used as the title of a foxtrot.

Many children's games include potatoes. In 'Pass the Potato', for instance, children stand in a circle with their hands behind their backs and pass a potato around the circle. 'Hot Potato' is a children's game similar to musical chairs. Its name derives from the expression 'like a hot potato', referring to something that is metaphorically 'dropped' – for instance, an erstwhile friend who turns out to be less than desirable. This first appeared, according to the OED, in 1821, and it's had staying power, remaining part of our slang almost two centuries later.

In 1952 a novel plaything, Mr Potato Head, arrived on the market. Created by George Lerner of Brooklyn, New York, it was manufactured by a small company called Hassenfeld Brothers. The Mr Potato Head toy was a set of prong-backed, cartoonish plastic facial features (eyes, ears, noses, mouths, eyebrows and moustaches), arms and legs that were intended be stuck into a real potato to create a man (like Eve, Mrs Potato Head came along later). The use of a real potato as a plaything was seen as wasteful, and it ran against the maternal injunction not to 'play with your food'. So in 1964 a plastic potato became part of the Mr Potato Head kit, and the pleasure of randomly sticking those funny features into a knobby, bulbous, real potato – which brought its own 'features' to the experience – was gone for good.

Since then, potato heads have survived and thrived in a variety of new dimensions from its movie debut in *Toy Story*,

uss *Iowa*, peeling spuds.

and the popular American movie spin-off 'Hasbro Mr Potato Head Spider-Man & Friends Spider Spud', to the macabre 'Mr Potato Head Executioner' patches, mouse pads, key chains, aprons, greeting cards and shirts, which are popular in England. Mr and Mrs Potato Head are alive and well in the literary and cultural world as they are featured in a variety of children's books, such as *Mr and Mrs Potato Head Go On Vacation* (2001) and *Mr Potato Head's Busy Day* (2008).

The potato's playfulness was not limited to Mr Potato Head. During the Second World War the Royal Navy developed the Holman Projector, which shot projectiles, such as grenades, several hundred feet using compressed air. After the war, hobbyists applied the concept using compressed air and potatoes as the ammunition. These devices were variously called spudguns, potato guns or potato cannons. These come in various sizes from small guns which shoot small pieces of potato to large ones that fire the complete potato. Spudguns are available for sale, or they can be made in the home. In 1993 the spudgun moved into the commercial world, when an inventor patented a gun that shot small chunks of flash-frozen potato to remove paint from buildings.

The Musical Potato

The potato has made it into records, on stage, and in book and film titles. In 1927 the jazz trumpeter Louis Armstrong recorded 'Potato Head Blues'. In 1934 R. C. Walsh wrote a comedy titled the 'Potato Salad King', and in the 1950s Peter Kennedy and Ann Driver produced a film, *One Potato, Two Potato*, which was released by the British Film Institute. In the 1970s, Mary and Herbert Knapp published *One Potato, Two Potato . . . the Secret Education of American Children*, which looked at the influence of games and play on child development.

Pop vocalist Dee Dee Sharp's top-selling record 'It's Mashed Potato Time' hit the airwaves on 5 May 1962. The Mashed Potato was a new dance, something like the Twist but with the addition of 'mashing' foot movements. It hit #4 on Billboard's chart seven weeks later. Sharp, a Philadelphia girl, appeared on the popular television show American Bandstand to lip-synch the new song.

Potato Politics

You wouldn't think that the spelling of a vegetable would make much of a ripple in US politics, and surely not that it would wreak havoc with a presidential campaign, but the potato has that dubious distinction. On 15 June 1992 George

Ginou Choueiri, *Potato Portraits*, 2009. Lebanese artist Choueiri uses potatoes because of their similarities to human skin colour and texture, and to symbolize growth, aging and decay.

Bush and Dan Quayle, the incumbent president and vice-president, were revving up their re-election campaign, when Dan Quayle walked into a classroom at the Munoz-Rivera Elementary School in Trenton, New Jersey. Quayle was set to moderate a spelling bee as part of the Bush–Quayle campaign. He read out the word 'potato' for twelve-year-old contestant William Figueroa, who was asked to write it on the chalk board. Figueroa spelled it correctly. Quayle looked at his contest card, where for some reason an 'e' had been appended to the end of the word. He gently hinted to the boy, 'You're close, but you left a little something off . . . the "e" on the end.' Figueroa went back to the board and dutifully added an 'e'.

Nobody said anything until the press conference following the spelling bee, when a reporter asked Quayle, 'How do you spell potato?' and everyone burst out laughing.

The editors at the local newspaper, *The Trentonian*, thought the spelling error was a good story and interviewed Figueroa, who called the Vice President an 'idiot'. This comment put the story on the front page, with the banner headline reading, 'Dan Can't Spell "Potato"'. The story made the evening news and appeared nationwide in newspapers during the following days. The story made the VP fair game for comedians; on his television show, David Letterman joked, 'I know he's not an idiot, but he needs to study more. Do you have to go to college to be vice president?'

William Figueroa was invited to appear on the Letterman Show, and that summer he led the Pledge of Allegiance at the Democratic National Convention. He marched in Trenton's Puerto Rican Day parade, and appeared on a talk show in Puerto Rico. Figueroa quickly became known in the US as 'The Potato Kid' and in Puerto Rico as 'el rey de la papa' – the Potato King.

The incident was, of course, dubbed 'Potatogate'. Five months later Bush and Quayle were defeated in their bid for re-election. Dan Quayle's error continued to haunt him throughout his life. In his 1994 memoir, *Standing Firm*, Quayle wrote an entire chapter about the incident. 'It was more than a gaffe. It was a "defining moment" of the worst imaginable kind. I can't overstate how discouraging and exasperating the whole event was.'

Potatoes have also played a role in international politics. In 2003 the French government refused to support the American-led effort in Iraq. In response, the US Representative Robert W. Ney, the Chair of the House Administration Committee, ordered all references to 'French fries' be expunged from the menus of the restaurants and snack bars run by the House of Representatives. French fries were renamed 'Freedom Fries'. In November 2006 Ney resigned from Congress when he pleaded guilty to charges of conspiracy and making false statements, and a few days later the name was quietly changed back to French fries.

.

7
The Global Potato Today and Tomorrow

Over the past fifty years, potato cultivation has increased throughout the world. For the past two decades, however, consumption of this nutritious vegetable in developed countries has declined. In part this is because people in those countries can afford more meat, poultry and fish, and no longer need to rely on starchy foods for sustenance. It may also be due to increased interest in health and fitness, especially the popularity of low-carbohydrate weight-loss diets. To the starch-averse dieter, the potato is just 'fattening' carbs; to the calorie- and fat-gram counters, many of the familiar potato 'formats' – chips or fries, scalloped or smothered in butter, salt and sour cream – are out of the question.

Today the majority of potatoes are grown and consumed in the developing world. In East Africa the potato has become a staple crop in mountainous areas of several countries, including Ethiopia, Uganda and Malawi; in Asia, it is a major crop in India, Bangladesh, Indonesia, Vietnam and China. Surprisingly, both cultivation and consumption have rapidly surged in two unlikely countries – China and India – where potatoes had not previously played much of a role in the local cuisines. Today, these two countries are respectively the world's largest and third largest potato producers and consumers.

The Asian Potato

It was likely Portuguese explorers who brought the potato to India on board their sailing vessels, although exactly when they did this is uncertain because of linguistic confusion. The term *potato* appears in India as early as 1615, but it is unclear whether this refers to the sweet potato, which most likely arrived first, or the common potato. The potato may also have arrived overland, perhaps from Turkey or Russia. In any case, in the eighteenth century the potato was a minor vegetable grown mostly in the kitchen gardens of British colonials. British colonial administrators did encourage potato cultivation in the late nineteenth century, but the varieties introduced during the Raj were unsuitable for the growing conditions in much of India. The exception was the higher altitudes in the north, where potato cultivation thrived during the Colonial period. The potato became a staple crop for many Sikhs and Punjabis, who dubbed it *aloo*, which derives from a generic Sanskrit word meaning an underground tuber.

Potato cultivation increased during the Second World War; it was easy and fast to grow and was filled with nutrition. By the time the war ended, potatoes had become a familiar item in the Indian diet. After Independence, in 1949, the Indian government established the Central Potato Research Institute (CPRI) to improve potato varieties, and production increased from 2.6 million tons in 1964 to 8.5 million tons in 1987. Today, most of the commercial crop is grown in Uttar Pradesh, West Bengal and Bihar. The 2008 harvest was expected to be more than 30 million tons, up 15 per cent from the previous year.

It comes as no surprise that many Indian recipes, especially those from the northern part of India such as the Punjab and Kashmir, make use of potatoes. Like many Indian

Utagawa Kuniyoshi, *I imo-hatake arashi*, from the series *Gedo juni-shi*, 1855, woodblock print showing a servant from a farming household driving 'boars' off land as they scavenge for potatoes.

dishes, some of the preparations are spicy, flavoured with cumin, coriander, mustard seeds and chillies. There are a great number of regional potato dishes, such as Kashmir's *dum aloo* (boiled potatoes simmered in a yogurt sauce), and Punjab's rustic *aloo gobi* (potatoes and cauliflower) and *aloo muttar* (potatoes and peas). Punjab is also home to *aloo paratha* – a flatbread stuffed with potatoes. Other popular Punjabi recipes include *aloo dum pukht* (slow-cooked potatoes). In south India, snack foods such as *masala dosa* (a large crêpe filled with spiced potatoes) and potato-and-vegetable-filled *pakoras* (fried turnovers) are popular. Pakoras are also common in Pakistan, Bengal and Afghanistan.

The state of Gujarat is home to sweet-and-sour potato curries flavoured with tomatoes, tamarind and jaggery (coarse brown sugar). Both in Gujarat and further south in Maharashtra, potatoes are pan-fried with peanuts and rice flakes.

Tractor planting potatoes on a potato farm.

There are also many Anglo-Indian *aloo* dishes, such as vegetarian chops, cutlets and patties, which are favoured by Mumbai housewives.[11]

It is most likely that the Dutch introduced the potato into China after 1600. It was grown in mountainous areas of northern and western China, but was not of much importance until the early twentieth century, when new varieties of high-yielding potatoes and new technologies for harvesting and processing them increased the crop. The Chinese government began potato experimentation in 1914, and improved varieties and advanced breeding methods were introduced. Potatoes became an important crop in China during the Second World War, when nationalists and communists – as well as the invading Japanese – saw the advantages of a foodstuff that was easy to grow, could be stored for a few months and was easy to transport.

After the war, potato planting dramatically increased throughout China, especially in Guizhou, Ganzu, Inner Mongolia, Yunnan and Sichuan. Even in the warmer climate of southern China, potatoes could be grown over the winter. By 1950 production had reached 8.7 million tons. As potatoes became a staple crop, the government invested in research and the development of new varieties. By 1980 China was producing 24.6 million tons of potatoes.

Production was further spurred by additional massive investments in potato research: by 1990 China funded four national potato research institutes, twenty agricultural academies and many hundreds of projects. More than 250 new potato varieties were developed for a variety of commercial uses. Processing facilities with advanced technology were established by importing twenty potato production lines for manufacturing potato starch, chips, fries and flakes. In addition, Simplot and PepsiCo opened facilities in China to support the growing needs of fast-food establishments, which flooded into China beginning in the 1990s. Today 130 plants process 2.3 million tons of raw potatoes into French fries, mashed potatoes and potato chips, which have become increasingly popular with Chinese consumers.

Virtually all the potatoes grown in China are eaten there. Although most of the dishes are unfamiliar to Westerners, the potato plays an important role in the Chinese diet. Many Chinese cookbooks contain recipes for potatoes, such as fried potatoes with pepper sauce, potato noodles, green pepper potato shreds and sautéed potatoes, eggplant (aubergine) and pepper.

By 2006 China's potato production increased to 74 million tons, the largest in the world. Today the potato is one of seven major Chinese crops, and the Chinese consume 88 lb (40 kg) per person annually. Potato production could easily increase by 30 per cent in the near future.

Potato Research

In addition to the geographical diversification of the potato, it has also been at the forefront of scientific developments. Humans have been altering the genetic make-up of plants and animals for thousands of years. Genetic mutations occur naturally in all living organisms, and when such mutations were seen as beneficial, these advantages were reinforced though selective breeding. It took years – sometimes centuries – to develop the forerunners of today's food plants and domesticated animals. This process was sped up in the late nineteenth century with the application of scientific methods to breeding. Potato research centres were launched in many countries in Europe and North America. Plant scientists had refined the technique of potato breeding, resulting in many new productive varieties.

Potato research took a major positive turn due to Nicolai Vavilov, a Russian agricultural botanist, who theorized that wild relatives of domesticated food crops might have useful genetic elements that could improve disease resistance or some other beneficial trait. In 1920 he was charged with improving the food crops in the Soviet Union. Due to the disruptions caused by the Russian Revolution in 1917, famine stalked the Soviet Union and by 1921, an estimated five million people had died as a result of starvation or diseases exacerbated by hunger. Vavilov's work became a high priority and the Soviet Union funded his travels to collect wild specimens from countries around the world. Due to the importance of potatoes in the Soviet Union, Vavilov visited South America, where he collected numerous wild potato varieties. Research and experiment centres in the Soviet Union commenced major efforts, and potato research escalated using the specimens Vavilov had collected.

Vavilov's work stimulated potato research outside the Soviet Union. Virtually every major potato-producing country has run experiments, established centres for potato breeding and improvement and helped disseminate better potato varieties. In 1972 a cooperative venture between foundations and governments formed the International Potato Center (CIP) in La Molina, outside of Lima, Peru, to reduce poverty and achieve food security on a sustained basis in developing countries through scientific research and related activities focusing on the potato and other root crops. The CIP maintains almost five thousand potato accessions, including about one hundred wild species. During the past decades, CIP has accelerated the introduction of improved potato varieties and supporting technologies throughout the developing world. It is funded by the World Bank, the UN, governments, foundations and non-governmental organizations.

Genetically Modified Potatoes

In the mid-twentieth century, a very different way of modifying plants and animals arose from the pioneering work of Cambridge University scientists James Watson and Francis Crick, who deciphered the structure of the DNA molecule, discovering that it formed a double helix. In 1953 Watson and Crick submitted a one-page paper to the British journal *Nature* describing their discovery. The paper closed with the observation, 'It has not escaped our notice that the specific pairing that we have postulated immediately suggests a possible copying mechanism for the genetic material.' By the 1980s, commercial applications for the new technology were explored – first for pharmaceuticals, and then for agricultural products.

Sequencing of the complete potato genome, usually the first step in genetic engineering, is under way, and is expected to be completed by the end of 2010. It will increase knowledge and understanding of genetic interactions and functional traits. However, even before the mapping of the potato's genes has been completed, scientists have already begun to genetically modify the plant. BASF, the German chemical giant, began working on genetically modified potatoes in 1998. The result was *Amflora*, a genetically modified potato rich in starch. It is intended for industrial uses and animal feed. It is currently under consideration for approval by the European Union.

Both India and China have poured resources into the development of genetically modified potatoes. In 2002 scientists

Illustration of a potato beetle on a plant.

The life cycle of a Colorado beetle.

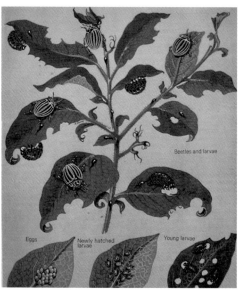

Beetles and larvae

Eggs

Newly hatched larvae

Young larvae

at Jawaharlal Nehru University in Delhi inserted a gene called 'AmA1' into the potato, which added one-third more protein than the conventional potato. They called their creation the *protato*. In mainly vegetarian India, where protein intake is limited, this could well lead to improved nutrition for the

Colorado potato beetle larvae.

nation's poor. As of 2009, however, the protato has not been approved for general dissemination.

Other genetically modified potato varieties include Monsanto's 'New Leaf' lines, which confer a resistance to viruses and the Colorado potato beetle. These were released in Canada and the United States in the 1990s. Due to public pressure against the use of genetically modified foods, several large commercial potato users, such as McDonald's, Burger King, Frito-Lay and Proctor & Gamble refused to use genetically modified potatoes, and Monsanto stopped producing them.

International Year of the Potato

In 2005 the Food and Agriculture Organization requested that the United Nations declare 2008 the 'International Year of the Potato'. The year was filled with conferences on the humble spud, and many technical works on the potato and its diseases were published, as were popular books, such as

John Reader's excellent *Propitious Esculent: The Potato in World History* (2008). The IYP also saw the publication of a wide variety of cookbooks, including *How the Chinese Eat the Potato* by Dongu yu Qu and Kaiyun Xie, which includes hundreds of potato recipes from each region of China as well as a few recipes for 'Western Style Potato Dishes', and *Potatoes* by Tarla Dalal, one of India's best selling cookbook authors. Her book contains more than a hundred recipes for Indian *aloo* dishes – salads, kofta, poshto, curries, gravies and soups – as well as an assortment of 'International Potato Dishes', including 'Chinese Style Potato Vegetables' and rösti. Other cookbooks published in 2008 include *Potato: 150 Fabulous Recipes* by Alex Barker and Sally Mansfield, and Florence Lebras's *The Potato Around the Globe in 200 Recipes: An International Cookbook*, which was published by the United Nations.

The Future

During the next two decades the world's population is expected to grow by an average of more than 100 million a year. More than 95 per cent of the increase will occur in developing countries, where pressure on land, water and other resources is already intense. Feeding an estimated nine billion people is a daunting prospect.

During the past fifty years, potato production in developing countries worldwide has increased more than any other crop. The potato is one of the most important commodities in the world. It is grown commercially in more than 130 countries, with annual production exceeding 320 million tons. It is a staple food for more than 1 billion people. Potatoes account for a huge proportion of the fresh produce trade in the world and are important components of the fast-food and snack-food industries. Potatoes are a mainstay of cuisines in both the developed and the developing world, and source of livelihood for millions of people. It is extremely likely that the potato will play an ever-increasing role in our future food supply.

Recipes

Historical Recipes

Potato Cake
—from Charles Elmé Francatelli, *The Modern Cook: A Practical Guide to the Culinary Art in All its Branches* (London, 1846)

Bake eighteen large York potatoes, and when done, rub their pulp through a wire sieve; put this into a large basin, add four ounces of butter, eight ounces of sifted sugar, a spoonful of pounded vanilla, a gill of cream, the yolks of six eggs and the whipped whites of two, and a little salt; work the whole well together, and then place it in a mould previously spread with butter, and strewn with bread crumbs; bake the cake for about an hour, and when done, dish it up with a fruit sauce poured round the base, made in the following manner:

Pick one pound of either currants, raspberries, cherries, damsons, strawberries, or apricots; place them in a stewpan with eight ounces of sifted sugar and half a gill of water; boil the whole down to the consistency of a thick pureé, and then rub it through a sieve or tammy.

Pommes de Terre Souflées (Puffed Potatoes)

—from François Tanty, *La Cuisine François* (Chicago, IL, 1893)

Proportions. —For five persons:
Potatoes . . . 12
Fat . . . Enough to fry.
Salt . . . to taste.

Preparation. 1st. Peel the potatoes, cut them endwise in slices about ¼ inch thick. 2d. Put them in warm but not hot fat. Let them cook till tender (10 minutes) 3d. Take the potatoes from the fat, let them drip and put them aside. 4th. Heat the fat very hot and pour the potatoes in it again, and fry quickly. They will puff and have a very nice appearance.

Potato Scallop

—from Mrs W. J. Bunton, Appleby, Ontario, in the *Canadian Farm Cook Book* (Toronto, 1911)

Grease a deep pudding dish and place in the bottom a layer of potatoes, peeled, and sliced very thin; next, a layer of thin sliced onions, then a layer of bread crumbs; sprinkle some pepper over this and a little pinch of salt; next, layer of potatoes, and repeat until the dish is full, having the potatoes on top. Cover with sweet milk and bake in a hot oven for an hour, or until the potatoes can be pierced with a fork.

Modern Recipes

The Best (and Quickest) Mashed Potatoes
—contributed by Ken Albala, professor of history, University of
the Pacific, Stockton, California

Take four large russet potatoes and poke several times with a
paring knife. Put them in the microwave on full power for 10
minutes. Check to see if soft and cooked through, if not, cook
a further 4 or 5 minutes. When done, and while still hot, remove
from microwave and cut in half. Place a half cut side down into
a ricer and press down firmly. Repeat with all the potato halves,
removing skin from ricer when necessary. Add two pats of butter, several pinches of salt and a good pour of milk until desired
consistency is achieved. Stir and serve immediately. For extra
flourish add some freshly grated parmigiano reggiano and a dash
of truffle oil.
Serves 4

Stir-Fried Potatoes and Cauliflower (Aloo Gobee)
—contributed by Veronica Sidhu, author of *Menus and Memories from
Punjab: Meals to Nourish Body and Soul* (New York, 2009)

This dish, because of its mild flavour and spicing, is a favourite
of Indian kids. To make it even milder leave out the mustard seed
or garam masala entirely and/or the whole cumin, or add more
heat in the form of a half-teaspoon of cayenne pepper. If you
like your cauliflower somewhat browned in spots, don't use the
microwave or a nonstick wok and just use a little more oil (and
time) to fry it.

1 medium/large cauliflower, washed and trimmed
⅓ cup canola or vegetable oil
1 teaspoon black mustard seeds (optional)

1 medium onion, sliced fine
1 teaspoon ground or whole cumin seeds (optional)
2 teaspoons ground turmeric
1 teaspoon crushed coriander seeds
1 teaspoon garam masala, divided (optional)
2 cloves garlic, minced
2 inch (5 cm) piece ginger, grated
3 large red potatoes, peeled and cubed into 1-inch pieces
1 ½ teaspoons salt, or more to taste
¼ cup sliced fresh cilantro [coriander] leaves

Break the cauliflower into florets and cut the stem into small pieces. Slice the nicer green leaves. Pour ¼ cup (60 ml) water into a microwavable dish or bowl. Add the cauliflower leaves, stems and florets. Cover and microwave for 5–6 minutes on high.

In a large wok, heat the oil over medium heat. Add the mustard seeds first and stir-fry for 30 seconds until they 'pop'. Add the onion and lightly brown. Add the cumin, turmeric, coriander seeds, ½ teaspoon garam masala, garlic and ginger. Fry for another 1–2 minutes. Add the potatoes, and stir-fry until they are evenly coated with spices. Cover and cook over low heat for 5 minutes, stirring once. Add the drained cauliflower. Sprinkle with the salt. Mix thoroughly, stir-frying vigorously over high heat for at least 5 minutes, adding more oil if necessary, until all the spices are evenly distributed and the cauliflower is browned, if desired.

Turn down the heat and finish cooking until tender, about 10 minutes if you microwaved the cauliflower. Stir-fry uncovered (if you like your vegetables dry) or covering (if you like them wetter). Sprinkle with the remaining ½ teaspoon of garam masala and garnish with cilantro before serving.
Serves 8

Tomato-Chèvre-Potato Frittata

—contributed by Bonnie Tandy Leblang, internationally syndicated
food columnist, cookbook author and blogger. For more information,
go to her website, www.BiteoftheBest.com.

½ lb/ 225 g Yukon gold potatoes
3 shallots, minced
6 eggs
salt
freshly ground black pepper to taste
4 oz/ 115 g chèvre (soft goat cheese), crumbled
¼ cup/25 g grated Parmesan
2 medium-sized ripe tomatoes, sliced

Cook potatoes in boiling salted water for 5–7 minutes until tender; drain. (This can be done the night before.) Cook in 2 teaspoons each of butter and olive oil in a medium heavy-bottomed skillet with an ovenproof handle over medium-high heat until the potatoes are golden, about 5–7 minutes. Add shallots and cook until softened, about 2 minutes. Meanwhile, beat eggs, 1 tablespoon water, some salt and lots of pepper together in a bowl; stir in chèvre and 2 tablespoons Parmesan cheese. Gently stir eggs into skillet. Lay tomato slices on top of eggs; sprinkle with remaining Parmesan cheese. Cook 3 minutes or until almost set. Place under broiler until browned and puffed, about 2 minutes. Cut into wedges and serve.

Serves 4

Estilo Del Rancho De Mi Madre: Papas Con Chorizo
—contributed by Mary Lou Dantona

Ingredients:
3 medium potatoes (peeled and chopped into small pieces)
1 package of chorizo (pork or beef)
1 small jalapeno chilli (seeded and minced)
4 large eggs

Directions:
Remove skin and crumble chorizo into large skillet over medium heat. Add potatoes.

Add minced jalapenos. Simmer for 6–8 minutes until potatoes are soft. Beat eggs in medium bowl while potatoes and chorizo are cooking. Stir in eggs to potatoes and chorizo until done, but still moist. Serve with flour or corn tortillas.
Serves 4

Estilo Del Rancho Del Mi Padre: Papas Con Huevos
—contributed by Mary Lou Dantona

4 medium potatoes (peeled and chopped)
2 fresh medium tomatoes (chopped)
1 small garlic clove (chopped)
1 medium jalapeno chilli (seeded and minced)
⅓ cup (40 g) red onion (chopped)
⅓ cup (80 ml) canola or vegetable oil
6 large eggs

Cook oil, potatoes, onion, garlic and jalapeno in a large frying pan or skillet at light to medium heat until potatoes are browned. Whisk the eggs in a bowl and add to the pan. Stir all the ingredients together. Cook over a low heat for 3–4 minutes until egg is cooked. Serve immediately with salsa and flour or corn tortillas.
Serves 4

Tu Dou Si (Shredded Potatoes)
—contributed by Emi Kazuko via Deh-Ta Hsiung, co-author of
The Food of China: A Journey for Food Lovers (Vancouver, BC, 2005)

Peel two large potatoes, then cut them into matchstick-sized shreds. Wash under cold water to get rid of excess starch and drain well.

Stir-fry in hot oil with shredded ginger and garlic, add salt and a little vinegar and a few drops of sesame oil. Serve hot or cold. Most delicious!

Serves 4–6 as a side dish

Chorizo con Papa
—contributed by Rachel Laudan, author of *The Food of Paradise: Exploring Hawaii's Culinary Heritage*

Chorizo con papa is basically a kind of hash. You will find it all over Mexico, ready to be rolled up in soft corn tortillas or stuffed into gorditas with lettuce, onion and tomatoes. You can also eat it by itself though this is less traditional. It makes a wonderful breakfast.

½ lb (225 g) good-quality chorizo
1 large potato, peeled and cut into ½ inch cubes

Skin the sausage, place it in a frying pan, and break it apart with a spatula. Cook gently until the fat begins to flow. Add the potato, cover the pan and continue to cook until the potato is soft. (You can speed this up by using cold, cooked potato.) Remove the lid and mash everything together, allowing it to brown a bit. You should end up with crumbs of chorizo clinging to the pieces of potato. This makes enough for six tortillas or gorditas.

Serves 6

Dried Potato Pizza-type Pancake with Spinach, Meat and Egg Whites

—contributed by Jackie Newman, editor of *Flavor & Fortune*,
a quarterly publication of the Institute of the Science and Art of
Chinese Cuisine

1 lb (450 g) dried potato slices or shreds, soaked in warm water
for an hour, drained, the water squeezed out and discarded
2 tablespoons potato starch
1 teaspoon salt
¼ cup (60 ml) vegetable oil
¼ teaspoon ground Sichuan pepper or five-spice powder
3 tablespoons hand-shredded fresh or dried and reconstituted
beef
¼ lb (110 g) fresh spinach, shredded, then blanched for half
a minute, drained, all water squeezed out
1 egg white
salt and ground white pepper, to taste

Mix drained potato slices or shreds with the potato starch and
salt. Press these onto a plate formed into a circle.

Heat a wok or frying pan, add the oil, and slide the potato
pancake into the oil, frying until it is a light tan colour. Turn over
and fry the other side, remove from the pan and drain on a paper
or cloth towel, then cut into four to eight triangular sections, and
place on a serving plate, keeping it warm in an oven or wrapping
it in aluminium foil.

Reheat the oil. Mix the beef with the ground pepper and fry
it for one minute, add the spinach and stir-fry this mixture for 30
seconds, or until heated thoroughly.

Mix the egg white with salt and pepper and add it to the meat
mixture, being sure to keep the heat high. Stir-fry just until the
egg white sets. Then pour this over the potato and serve.

Yield: six cups

Chinese Potato Chip Dinner
—contributed by Jackie Newman, editor of *Flavor and Fortune*

1 lb (450 g) potatoes, peeled and sliced (can use reconsituted dried potato slices)
1 teaspoon coarse salt
1 teaspoon fermented black beans, smashed or chopped minimally
1 chilli pepper (seeded if wanting the dish less piquant), and minced
2 tablespoons vegetable oil
1 small tomato, coarsely chopped
1 teaspoon potato starch

Mix the potato slices with the salt, black beans and chilli. Heat a pan or wok, add oil, and then add potato mixture and fry for five minutes, stirring several times. Add chopped tomato and the potato starch and simmer until the potatoes are cooked to the desired firmness, about another minute, then serve.
Yield: four cups

Tattie Scones
—contributed by Nichola Fletcher, author of *Caviar: A Global History*

225 g (8 oz) hot boiled potato
pinch of salt
1 tablespoon butter
100 g (4 oz) plain (all-purpose) flour
extra flour if necessary

Mash the potato with the salt and butter. Turn it out onto a floured board. Knead the potato into the flour, working in enough to make a workable dough. Roll it out very thin (about 4 mm or ⅛ inch) and prick the dough with a fork. Cut it into two rounds, and cut each round into quarters. Cook for about 3 minutes each

side on a hot girdle* or flat frying pan. The scones should have a dark greyish-brown speckled surface. Serve as fresh as possible, spread with butter.
Makes 8

* A girdle was the traditional Scots method of cooking all forms of flat bread, scones, bannocks and oatcakes. It is a heavy, flat disk made of cast iron, with a handle that would hang over an open peat fire. It would be lightly greased before use.

Vinegrette (Russian Potato Salad)
—contributed by Tatiana Kling

This can be served as an appetizer (starter) or side dish.

2 cooked beets (beetroot) – canned are acceptable (diced)
4 boiled potatoes (diced)
2 dill pickles (diced)
¼ cup (60 ml) mayonnaise or 1 tablespoon oil
salt and pepper (to taste)
one sprig dill (chopped) and/or 2 scallions (spring onions) (chopped)
2 hard-boiled eggs (chopped finely)

Mix the cooked beets, potatoes and dill pickles (gherkins) in a large bowl. Mix in mayonnaise or oil. Add salt and pepper to taste, and the chopped pickles and/or chapped scallions (spring onions).

Mix completely and put into serving bowl; allow to chill for about 30 minutes. Garnish with chopped egg just before serving.
Serves 8–10

Potato and Mushroom Soup
—contributed by Tatiana Kling

4 tablespoons oil, margarine or butter
1 medium onion (chopped)
1 carrot (diced)
2 lbs (900 g) potatoes (peeled and diced)
6 cups (1400 ml) stock (chicken or vegetable)
1 teaspoon salt
1 bay leaf
1 teaspoon dried parsley
1 tsp dried dill (optional)
pepper to taste
½ cup (120 ml) sour cream
1 lb (450 g) mushrooms (sliced)
dill for garnish

Put half the oil, margarine or butter in a large pot and heat. Add onions and carrots. Sauté for about 5–6 minutes until the onions are translucent. Add the potatoes and stock. Add the salt, bay leaf, dried parsley, dried dill and pepper. Cover and cook for about 20 minutes until the potatoes are tender. Remove the bay leaf. Remove a cup of potatoes and purée them, then stir this purée back into the pot. Stir in the sour cream.

Fry the mushrooms in the remaining oil, margarine or butter until lightly browned and slightly crispy. Reserve some mushrooms for garnish. Add the remaining mushrooms to the soup and stir in.

Top each serving of soup with a small sprig of dill (or chopped dill) and crispy mushrooms.

Serves 6

Potato and Herring 'Torte'
—contributed by Tatiana Kling

This dish is eaten as an appetizer (starter).

5 boiled potatoes (chopped)
4 pickled herring fillets (chopped)
½ small onion (minced) divided into 2 portions
4 cooked beets (beetroot) (sliced), canned are fine
2 raw carrots (grated)
3 scallions (spring onions) (chopped), divided into 3 portions
4 hard-boiled eggs (chopped)
2 tablespoons mayonnaise divided into 2
salt and pepper to taste

Use a clear glass bowl or small platter. The ingredients will be layered.

In another bowl, mix boiled potatoes with 1 tablespoon of the mayonnaise and half of the chopped onion. Add salt and pepper to taste. Put the potato mixture in a glass bowl or on a platter. Put the chopped herring, mixed with the other half of the chopped onion, on top of the potato layer. Add the sliced beets, mixed with a third of the scallions, on top of herring layer. Put the grated carrots, mixed with another third of the scallions, on top of beet layer. Mix 1 tablespoon mayonnaise into the chopped eggs and use this as the final layer. Use the remaining scallions to garnish the top of the 'torte'. Refrigerate for an hour before serving.

References

1 The latest evidence suggests that the Americas may well have been settled thousands of years earlier.

2 *True Gentleman's Delight* as quoted in Thomas Wright, *Dictionary of Obsolete and Provincial English*, 2 vols (London, 1857), vol. II, p. 758.

3 William Salmon, *The Family Dictionary, or Household Companion* (London, 1695), p. 295.

4 I am indebted to Dr Thomas Gloning of the Institut für Germanistik, Justus-Liebig-Universität Gießen, for the information about early potato recipes in Germany.

5 Benjamin, Graf von Rumford, 'Essay of Food and Particularly on Feeding the Poor', *Essays, Political, Economical and Philosophical*, 3 vols (London, 1796).

6 Benjamin, Graf von Rumford, *The Complete Works of Count Rumford*, 5 vols (London, 1876), vol. V, p. 486.

7 Richard Bradley, *Two New and Curious Essays . . . To Which Is Annexed, the Various Ways of Preparing and Dressing Potatoes for the Table* (London, 1732), p. 62.

8 Benjamin, Graf von Rumford, 'Essay of Food and Particularly on Feeding the Poor', p. 125.

9 Ibid., p. 126.

10 William Ellis, *The Modern Husbandman, Or, the Practice of Farming*, vol. III (July–Sept.) (London, 1744), p. 119.

11 I am indebted to Veronica Sidhu, author of *Menus and Memories from Punjab: Meals to Nourish Body and Soul* (New

York, 2009), and Sejal Sukhadwala, food writer and editor, for their help on Indian recipes.

Select Bibliography

Bareham, Lindsey, *In Praise of the Potato: Recipes from around the World* (Woodstock, NY, 1992)

Bartoletti, Susan Campbell, *Black Potatoes: The Story of the Great Irish Famine, 1845–1850* (Boston, MA, 2001)

Bradshaw, John, and George Mackay, eds, *Potato Genetics* (Wallingford, 1994)

Burton, William Glynn, *The Potato* (Essex, 1989)

Correll, Donovan S., *The Potato and Its Wild Relatives* (Renner, TX, 1962)

Cullen, L. M., 'Irish History without the Potato', *Past and Present*, XL (July 1968), pp. 72–83

Curiæ, Amicus, *Food for the Million: Maize Against Potato: A Case for the Times, Comprising the History, Uses, & Culture of Indian Corn, and Especially Showing the Practicability and Necessity of Cultivating the Dwarf Varieties in England and Ireland* (London, 1847)

Davis, James W., *Aristocrat in Burlap: A History of the Potato in Idaho* [Boise]: Idaho Potato Commission, 1992.

Davis, Myrna, *The Potato Book* (New York, 1973)

Fagan, Brian M., *The Little Ice Age: How Climate Made History, 1300–1850* (New York, 2000)

Ferrières, Madeleine, trans. Jody Gladding, *Sacred Cow, Mad Cow: A History of Food Fears* (New York, 2006)

Foster, Elborg, and Robert Forster, eds, *European Diet from Pre-industrial to Modern Times* (New York, 1975)

Gilbert, Arthur W., Mortier Franklin Barrus, and Daniel Dean,

The Potato (New York, 1917)

Graves, Christine, ed., *The Potato Treasure of the Andes: from Agriculture to Culture* (Lima, 2001)

Grubb, E. H., and W. S. Guilford, *The Potato* (New York, 1912)

Guenthner, Joseph F. *The International Potato Industry* (Cambridge, 2001)

Hawkes, J. G., *The Potato: Evolution, Biodiversity and Genetic Resources* (Washington, DC, 1990)

—, and J. Francisco-Ortega, 'The Early History of the Potato in Europe', *Euphytica*, LXX (1993), pp. 1–7

—, 'Masters Memorial Lecture: The History of the Potato', *Journal of the Royal Horticultural Society*, Part 1 (1966), pp. 207–24; Part 2 (1966), pp. 248–62; Part 3 (1967), pp. 288–302

Johnson, George W., *The Potato: Its Culture, Uses, and History* (London, 1847)

Lang, James, *Notes of a Potato Watcher* (College Station, TX, 2001)

Laufer, Berthold, and C. Martin Wilbur, *The American Plant Migration; Part 1: The Potato* (Chicago, IL, 1938), vol. XXVIII

Linn, Biing-Hwan, Gary Lucier, Jane Allshouse and Linda S. Kantor, 'Market Distribution of Potato Products in the United States', *Journal of Food Products Marketing*, VI (2001), p. 4

Marshall, Lydie, *A Passion for Potatoes* (New York, 1992)

McIntosh, Thomas Pearson, *The Potato: Its History, Varieties, Culture and Diseases* (London, 1927)

McNeill, William H., 'The Introduction of the Potato into Ireland', *The Journal of Modern History*, XXI (September 1949), pp. 218–22

—, 'How the Potato Changed the World's History', in 'Food: Nature and Culture', *Social Research*, LXVI (Winter 1998), pp. 67–83

—, 'What if Pizzaro had Not Found Potatoes in Peru?' in *What If? Eminent Historians Imagine What Might Have Been*, ed. Robert Cowley (New York, 2001), vol. II, pp. 413–27

Reader, John, *Propitious Esculent: The Potato in World History* (London, 2008)

Rosen, Sherwin, 'Potato Paradoxes', *The Journal of Political Economy*, CVII, Part 2: Symposium on the Economic Analysis of Social Behavior in Honor of Gary S. Becker (December 1999), pp. S294–S313

Roze, Ernest, *Histoire de la Pomme de terre, traitée aux points de vue historique, biologique, pathologique, cultural, et utilitaire* (Paris, 1898)

Salaman, Redcliffe, *The History and Social Influence of the Potato* (Cambridge, 1949)

Sanders, T. W., *The Book of the Potato* (London, 1905)

Schlosser, Eric, *Fast Food Nation: The Dark Side of the All-American Meal* (Boston, MA, 2001)

Suttles, Wayne, 'The Early Diffusion of the Potato among the Coast Salish', *Southwestern Journal of Anthropology*, VII (Autumn 1951), pp. 272–88

Stuart, William, *The Potato: Its Culture, Uses, History and Classification* (Philadelphia, PA, and London, 1923)

Vreugdenhil, Dick, et al., ed., *Potato Biology and Biotechnology: Advances and Perspectives* (Oxford, 2007)

Whitney, Marylou [Mrs. Cornelius Vanderbilt Whitney], *The Potato Chip Cook Book* (Lexington, KY, 1977)

Wilson, Mary Tolford, 'Americans Learn to Grow the Irish Potato', *The New England Quarterly*, XXXII (September 1959), pp. 333–50

Woolfe, Jennifer A., with Susan V. Poats, *Potato in the Human Diet* (New York, 1987)

Zuckerman, Larry, *The Potato: How the Humble Spud Rescued the Western World* (Boston, MA, and London, 1998)

Websites and Associations

Potato Websites

British Potato Council
www.potato.org.uk

International Potato Center; Centro Internacional de la Papa
www.cipotato.org

Das Kartoffelmuseum (The Potato Museum, Munich)
www.kartoffelmuseum.de/museumseite.html

Thüringer Kloßmuseums Heichelheim
www.klossmuseum.de

Potato Association of America
http://potatoassociation.org

Potato Museum
www.potatomuseum.com/extpmhistory.html

European Cultivated Potato Database
www.europotato.org/menu.php?

International Year of the Potato
www.potato2008.org/en/index.html

PotatoPro
www.potatopro.com/

United States Potato Board (USPB)
www.potatoesusa.com, www.uspotatoes.com

Potato Associations

International Potato Center (CIP)

World Potato Congress Inc.

NORTH AMERICA

American Frozen Food Institute (AFFI)

Idaho Potato Commission

National Potato Council (NPC)

Northwest Food Processors Association

Packaging Machinery Manufacturers Institute (PMMI)

Potatoes New Brunswick (Canada)

Prince Edward Island Potato Board (Canada)

The Potato Association of America (PAA)

United States Potato Board

Washington State Potato Commission (WSPC)

SOUTH AMERICA

Associação Brasileira da Batata (Brazilian Potato Association)

Asociación Latinoamericana de la Papa (ALAP)
(Latin American Potato Association)

Fundacion PROINPA (Bolivia)

Instituto Nacional Autónomo de Investigaciones
Agropecuarias (INIAP, Ecuador)

Instituto Nacional de Tecnología Agropecuaria, INTA – Propapa
(Argentina)

EUROPE

Association des Amidonniers et Féculiers
(AAF; European Starch Association)

Belgapom
(Organization of Belgian Potato Processing companies)

Bundesverband der obst-, gemuese, und kartoffelverarbeitenden
Industrie (BOGK; the German Association for Processors of
Fruit, Vegetables and Potatoes)

Committee of the European Starch Potato Processors' Unions
(CESPU)

Dutch Potato Processing Association (DPPA or VAVI)

Europatat (represents the interests of wholesale potato
merchants at a European level) European Union

European Association for Potato Research (EAPR)

European Snacks Association (ESA)

Food and Drink Federation (FDF, UK)

Groupement Interprofessionnel pour la valorisation de la
Pomme de Terre (GIPT, France)

Navefri (Nationaal verbond van frituristen, national union of 'frituristen')

Nederlandse Aardappel Organisatie (NAO; Dutch Organisation of Potato Merchants)

Potato Council Limited (formerly known as British Potato Council, BPC)

Producers and Exporters Andalusian Early Potatoes (Spain)

Swisspatat (Switzerland)

UEITP (European Union of Potato Processors)

AUSTRALIA AND NEW ZEALAND

Australian Vegetable and Potato Growers Federation (AUSVEG)

The Chip Group (New Zealand)

Potato Processors Association Of Australia (PPAA)

Acknowledgements

Special thanks to Tom Hughes and Meredith Sayles Hughes of the Potato Museum in Albuquerque, New Mexico (http://www. potatomuseum.com) for their use of several illustrations from their collection, and special thanks to Mary Lou Dantona of Simi Valley, California, for her recipes for 'Papas Con Chorizo' and 'Papas Con Huevos', and her husband for his photograph of Mr Potato Head. I would also like to thank the following individuals who have supplied information about potatoes: Sejal Sukhadwala, food writer and editor, for help on Indian recipes; Nichola Fletcher, author of *Charlemagne's Tablecloth: A Piquant History of Feasting*, for the recipe for Tattie Scones; Dr Kenneth Albala, professor, University of the Pacific and author of numerous books on food history, for his recipe for mashed potatoes; Andrew Coe, author of *Chop Suey: a Cultural History of Chinese Food in the United States* (2009) for his help with Chinese potato recipes; Dr Jacqueline M. Newman, editor of *Flavor & Fortune*, a quarterly publication of the Institute of the Science and Art of Chinese Cuisine, for her recipe for 'Dried Potato Pizza-type Pancake with Spinach, Meat, and Egg Whites'; Veronica Sidhu, author of *Menus and Memories from Punjab: Meals to Nourish Body and Soul* (2009) for the recipe for 'Aloo Gobee'; Aylin Oney Tan for his help on the subject of the introduction of the potato into Turkey; Bonnie Tandy Leblang, an internationally syndicated food columnist, cookbook author and blogger, who contributed the recipe for 'Tomato-Chèvre-Potato Frittata'; Michael Krondl, for his information about the history of potatoes in the Czech Republic; Janet Clarkson of Brisbane for her comments regarding potatoes in Australia; and Thomas Gloning of the Institut für Germanistik, Justus-Liebig-Universität Gießen, for the information he supplied about early potato recipes in Germany. Permit me to especially thank Judy Gugeroy for her information on potatoes in Finland; and Carlton Bach of Hamburg, Germany, for his help with the history of German potatoes.

As usual, I'd like to thank Bonnie Slotnick for her help with editing this book. Her comments were invaluable. I'd also like to thank many researchers who contributed information for this book.

Photo Acknowledgements

The author and publishers wish to express their thanks to the following sources of illustrative material and/or permission to reproduce it:

Bigstock: p. 6 (Chris Leachman); © The Trustees of the British Museum: p. 104; Steve Caruso: p. 72 top; Fir0002/Flagstaffotos: p. 73; Istockphoto: p. 69 (Tomasz Parys) top right, 75 (Kelly Cline); Rhys James: p. 69 top left; Michael Leaman: p. 69 centre right; Library of Congress: pp. 22, 60, 97; The Metropolitan Museum of Art, New York, USA: p. 93 (Jacques and Natasha Gelman Collection, 998 (1999.363.50) Photographed by Malcolm Varon); Museum of Fine Arts, Boston, Massachussetts, USA: p. 92 bottom (Gift of Quincy Adams Shaw through Quincy A. Shaw, Jr and Mrs Marion Shaw Houghton 17.1505); National Cancer Institute, Bethesda, Maryland, USA: pp. 56, 64 (Renée Comet); National Library of Medicine, Bethesda, Maryland, USA: p.33, 88; The Potato Museum, Albuquerque, New Mexico, USA: pp. 12, 34, 95; Rex Features: pp. 8 (John Chapple), 62 (Denis Closon), 77 (Denis Closon), 83 (Sipa Press), 99 (Ginou Choueiri); Andrew F. Smith: p. 84; Stock Xchng: p. 74 (Alistair Williamson), 105 (Alan Rainbow), 111 (Jm2c); Man Vyi: p. 72 bottom; Swiatoslaw Wojtkowiak: p. 13; Rainer Zenz: p. 82.

Index